Living Stress Free

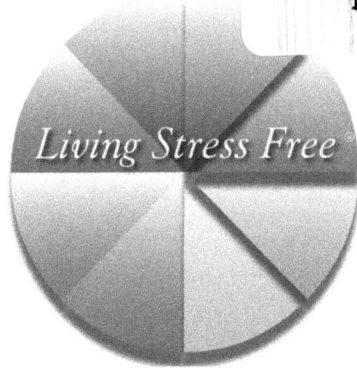

IT'S NEVER TOO LATE
TO DO NOTHING

Mindfulness Meditation, Yoga and Spiritual Intelligence

Louis J Guadagnino

Louis **Guadagnino**
Living Stress Free, Inc.
Rochester, New York

Dedicated to the Living Stress Free Community:
A community of caring people working to transition the ancient practices
of meditation and yoga into American culture.

Special thanks to Cyndi Moolekamp and to Eric Baart for their dedica-
tion and energy in all they do for the Living Stress Free Community.

CONTENTS

Chapter 2

Chapter 3

Chapter 4

Chapter 5

Chapter 6

Chapter 7

Chapter 8

Chapter 9

Chapter 10

Chapter 11

Chapter 16

PREFACE

Spirituality has been a significant part of my life since I was a little girl, taking different forms at different times. Throughout my childhood and adolescence, I embraced the religious traditions of my family and their ancestors, without hesitation. There was great honor and reverence in the path they followed and it brought me a sense of peace, devotion and purpose. My early experiences of a greatness beyond myself sowed the seeds for future exploration and insight, and I am grateful for this strong foundation.

As I entered my twenties, I had a yearning for something more. I was not satisfied with the relationship between religion and spirituality. There seemed to be a disconnect. I noticed I was much more interested in spirituality as a path itself, without the trappings of religion. By "trappings" I mean the inherent focus on dogma and belief as an expression of religion. I knew in my heart that spirituality is an experience, not a belief system. It exists beyond the realm of the thinking mind. I equated it to the feeling of love. Love is not something a person believes, it is an experience.

That began my search for a way to fully express spirituality in my life. I kept an open mind, I spent a lot of time in nature, and I read different ideas and philosophies on the subject. But most importantly, I spent time with different people who had various ways of expressing spirituality in their lives. People are fascinating to me and I am always curious to learn more from others.

In 1991, I met the single most significant person who helped shape my spiritual framework for the rest of my life. I found how to express my spirituality through my inner experience and allow this to spontaneously expand out of me to whomever I was with, amidst whatever I was doing. This person was not a priest or a rabbi. He was not a guru or a meditation master. He was not a college professor or a therapist. He was a coworker of mine, who later became my husband.

Lou Guadagnino started his spiritual journey at a young age. He had a difficult childhood with many painful challenges. He was not a stranger to suffering. He had a deep yearning to find out more about meditation, yoga and different religious and spiritual paths, partly as a way to cope with his difficulties but mostly as a meaningful quest. He began a relentless study on this subject starting at age thirteen. He delved into both eastern and western religious philosophies and practices.

What I find unique about Lou is that he was never satisfied with just an intellectual understanding of these religious and spiritual practices. He had to practice them fully, to experience them fully. The only way to truly learn something is to have both knowledge and experience. Through his need for experiencing the practices, he began to see there was a difference between religion and spirituality. One was in the mind, the other was universal.

Life, being the dance between pairs of opposites, always has a sense of irony. In the midst of the great experiences Lou was deriving from his spiritual journey, he was also trying to deal with the debilitating effects of post traumatic stress disorder. Panic attacks, depression and feelings of unworthiness were overpowering at times, affecting his functioning. He tried the traditional ways of treating these symptoms, with no relief. It was through this experience of suffering he learned the powerful healing effects of meditation.

Meditation was the answer for eliminating Lou's PTSD symptoms. Not only was it the key to enhancing spiritual experiences, it was the foundation for self growth, healing and recovery. Lou's mindfulness meditation practice taught him not to resist the panic attacks, but to fully experience them as part of his moment by moment open awareness. This changed his relationship with the symptom and allowed the habitual response to dissipate until one day it never returned. He discovered firsthand how a simple practice that basically consists of doing nothing can not only transform a person's spiritual life, it can heal imbalances and improve all aspects of life. It's never too late to do nothing!

After learning different spiritual practices and studying under various meditation masters through the years, it became clear to Lou that the place one arrived when going beyond the mind, the emotions, the ego was the same experience no matter which path was used. And because this is true, there is great potential for anyone, from any culture, race or religion, to experience that state for their own well being and transformation. This is the basis for Secular Spirituality.

Lou has practiced meditation for over forty years. He has had the good fortune to receive meditation instruction and guidance under recognized Buddhist and Yogic meditation masters. He has studied and practiced in the Zen and Vajrayana Buddhist traditions and in Tantric and Bhakti Yoga traditions. He was given permission to teach meditation from a recognized Tibetan meditation master.

His lifelong goal is to assist the cultural transition of Buddhist and Yogic Meditation into Western culture. He wrote It's Never Too Late To Do Nothing for this purpose. The teachings he learned and experienced throughout his life are universal. Not only do they support spiritual fulfillment, they cultivate a sense of well being, self reliance and personal growth. They are the secret to success. This is a whole new model of wellness.

Lou's style of writing may sound confrontational at times. To avoid any misunderstanding, allow me to explain his reasoning. He is not against any religion and has the utmost respect for all religious and spiritual paths. He has practiced many of these paths himself. The knowledge he is sharing in this book is inclusive to all paths, not exclusive to a certain religious group. Recognizing this universality is the source of Lou's rather direct tone when commenting on this subject. One of the main points of this book is the fact there is a universal spirituality available to each and every one of us outside of religion but also within religion. This awareness can be transformational and can help neutralize the destructive effects of "us and them" mentality. This is the essence of Secular Spirituality.

When I met Lou in 1991, I was searching for a way to deepen my connection to something greater, something beyond my limited ego with its habitual thoughts, feelings and behaviors that were keeping me stuck. He introduced me to the practice of mindfulness meditation, to the wisdom of the Buddhist and Yogic teachings, and to the practical application of this ancient knowledge. I watched my life slowly transform as I embraced these practices. I was less bothered by what other people thought about me. I did not get as stressed about mishaps and inconveniences. I felt causeless happiness and expanding love throughout my day, that resulted in contentment and inner peace. I became a better listener, a better therapist. I didn't have to plan any type of response to anyone. I naturally knew what to say. The knowledge and experience of the ancient teachings I have had the good fortune of discovering has transformed every area of my life.

Lou's ability to describe what he has learned and how to access this knowledge through It's Never Too late To Do Nothing is practical yet profound. After reading and practicing the tools given in this book, you will see aspects of your life improve as well. This is a new model of transformative personal growth. Enjoy the journey.

Marilyn Guadagnino MTBC, LCAT

Marilyn is a licensed psychotherapist, licensed creative arts therapist, certified music therapist and mindfulness meditation teacher. She has worked in community mental health since 1988 and has her own private psychotherapy practice in Rochester, NY. She has been meditating since 1992 and created and recorded a music and sound restorative technique called Nada Relaxation. Lou and Marilyn are the owners of Living Stress Free, Inc and offer classes, workshops and social events at the Living Stress Free Wellness Center, Rochester, NY. Learn more at livingstressfree.org

My Meditation Journey

Forty-five years ago I became interested in meditation. I read any book I could find on the subject. I read Hindu scriptures like Bhagavad Gita, books on yogis and enlightened masters such as Ramana Maharshi, commentators and philosophers like Alan Watts and people who helped transplant Yoga and Buddhism into American soil like Ram Dass and Philip Kapleau.

Meditation was a big part of American culture at the time and there were a number of growing groups across the states that represented different schools and traditions.

I loved them all. The simplicity of Zen, the unique method of using devotion to reach enlightenment in Bhakti Yoga, the tantric transformation of the details of everyday life in Vajrayana Buddhism and Shivaism, and the benefits of learning to perform selfless service in Karma Yoga.

I did my best to visit communities of each tradition. I usually practiced with them for a couple of years, although I spent more than a decade with some. I never intended to keep moving from one community to another or from one teacher to another. This is just what happened.

I chanted with the Hare Krishnas. I meditated with Yogis and Meditation Masters, practiced Zazen with Roshis, and studied under Gurus. They all did only good for me.

The people I met were always wonderful, despite the tendency towards a sense of snobbery amongst the senior American students in each tradition. Old habits die hard, I guess.

Years later, I married my wife Marilyn and together we encouraged each other's spiritual practices and growth. We also shared many experiences in several spiritual communities. Most of our memories are happy ones. It was liberating to meet people who genuinely cared, treated life as sacred, and were willing to learn about themselves, each other and life.

Through my experiences with the different spiritual communities I practiced with, I began to realize one of the most distinguishing contrasts between spirituality and religion. When it comes to religion, most people believe they already know everything they need to know. When it comes to spirituality, people seem to be humbled by the limitations of human thoughts and beliefs. They are able to voice the truth and say out loud what we all secretly know in our hearts to be humanly true: we really do not know anything, especially about God or the infinite. This realization was the catalyst for writing this book.

This Book is for You

When I entered the world of yoga and meditation life went topsy-turvy. Everything I usually considered vitally important, such as my thoughts and emotions, suddenly took a backseat to inner silence and awareness. For the first time in my life, consciousness was the center of my attention and not all the things I was conscious of.

As I became more aware of the silence within myself - what I call "Observing Awareness" - I began realizing an entire new way of perceiving and experiencing life. I also recognized that this inner perceptual shift wasn't only possible for me, it was possible for everyone! It is our birthright.

This book is about you. This book is for you. This is because we all share the same human predicament. At our core we are pure Observing Awareness, unbounded awareness and silence, and yet each of us is tangled up in what seems to be an unending chain of conflicts.

Some of these conflicts are about ourselves, such as how we think and feel about who we are. We may have an exaggerated idea of our importance and capabilities or we may not be able to see our goodness or our talents at all.

Some of these conflicts involve our relationships with family, friends, spouses, children and coworkers. Instead of these relationships being mutually nurturing, supportive and loving, they are marred with disappointments, dissatisfaction, gossip, blame and defensiveness.

Few of us recognize that our problems and conflicts are simply products of how we perceive things; they are colored by our thoughts, interpretations and beliefs. Our thoughts and emotions hold so much power over us because we never experience anything beyond them. We are prisoners of mind.

Many of us who do recognize that our thoughts and interpretations are causing us unnecessary complications and pain make the understandable mistake of trying to replace our problematic thoughts with new thoughts.

Many therapists, teachers, and motivational speakers encourage us to change our lives by changing our thoughts. Although in some ways this is good advice, what we eventually learn is that the mind that created our conflicts and troubles cannot fix them. Nothing makes this point clearer than our current world situation - a virtual battlefield of human thought.

Tradition versus Progression

I can't help but notice that the changes in the world we live in, as a result of progress in the fields of technology and science, appear to have deteriorated our collective understanding of the process of existence. Our old models of who we are and what life is all about are becoming obsolete.

This is really the crux of what I see in the world today. Our knowledge base has surpassed our archaic beliefs about ourselves and how to live, and society is reacting to this dilemma in different unconscious ways. Many people are demanding a return to the past as if we simply can forget or ignore what has been learned.

Fundamentalist religions and rigid narrow political philosophies hope to put the proverbial "skunk back in the box and pretend nobody smelled it." But their mission is hopeless. Progress is inevitable. Science and technology will continue to expand.

As we straddle the gulf between old religious and political models and a future that will undoubtedly include new models - models that embrace science and social progress - I feel strongly that we face a crushing spiritual crisis.

Most of what we thought we "knew" about ourselves, humanity, our shared history and destiny, turns out to be nothing more than organized belief systems. Our understanding of creation, the value of different species of life on our planet and the significance of the different roles that they play, our life purpose, and our perception of God, turn out to be virtually only thoughts in our heads or words we speak. This is the inherent problem with belief-based systems.

It is strange because if you ask people: "As your personal doctor, would you prefer a physician who recently graduated medical school or one who was educated while Jesus walked the earth?" Most would immediately choose a contemporary physician because they acknowledge scientific and social progress.

But when it comes to philosophy, religion, and all the human needs these fields attempt to address, we place our faith in information that is thousands of years old but is neither historical or scientific. In other words, we guard our bodies vigilantly but we throw our souls to the winds of tradition and chance.

It seems that those who most adamantly quote enlightened souls such as Jesus have never experienced what he and others like him are trying to convey. They are religious academics spiced up with a lot of passion. They can quote their holy book all day long on any subject but they are like tour guides who have only read about the faraway places they want to guide us through.

This isn't anyone's fault. This is how the human species evolves. First, a few special beings catch a glimpse of a new world, a new horizon for all of us, and many simply follow, hoping for a better life. Eventually, the new world that only a few grasped out of their own experience and knowledge spreads throughout humanity. As this shift of progress is occurring, chaos, upheaval, and conflicts break out. This is what we are seeing today when we look at the world around us.

Jesus, Buddha, Krishna, Lao-Tzu, Meher Baba and many others were sharing their personal experiences with those around them. They spoke and taught using the common symbols of their cultures and times. The reason we still learn about them, honor them and appreciate them, building communities around their words, is because of their universal and eternal messages.

I have learned that we too can experience what they experienced. We too can know what they know. When Jesus said, "The kingdom of heaven is within you," he meant that at your core, your deepest level of being, you *are* the kingdom of heaven. His words were not intended to be an article of faith. They were meant to point you in the right direction: inward.

Unfortunately, religious traditions - the very ones that we grew up learning, believing, and trying to put into practice - were not designed to encourage wisdom through spiritual practices or knowledge. They were designed to convert us to believing a very specific set of beliefs which manifest as a very specific lifestyle and worldview.

Jesus's words, for example, are usually not studied as a way of advancing personal experience of the 'kingdom of heaven within you' as they should be. They are taught as doctrine: words that explain reality and offer a precise worldview which a believer holds to be true and tries to live. Usually under the threat of eternal damnation!

The Problem with Thought

I have discovered that the reason for this emphasis on correct belief in faith-based religions is due to most people's lack of insight into the human mind. The mind, what I call "Active Mind," consists of thoughts, emotions, sensory experiences, Perceptual Awareness[1]and dreams.

However, all of these mind-things spring from thoughts. If mind was an engine, thinking would be oil. When we smell a flower we do not simply inhale its fragrance. It's odor is filtered through a vast

---

[1] Perceptual Awareness, Observing Awareness, Meditation Awareness, Active Mind, Crazy Mind and Spiritual Intelligence are all terms used in LSF to describe unique processes that pertain to meditation and yoga. They are capitalized throughout this book to make their individual meanings and their overall relationships to one another clearer to the reader.

filing system of our past experiences with flowers, odors, and much more, all coming together in the form of thoughts about those things.

No matter what we are experiencing in this world, we are experiencing our thoughts about it. In this way we are always living in the past. We taste soup, compare it with our past experiences of soup, and we react to the soup based on our thoughts from past experiences. The experiences themselves are gone. Only our thoughts about them remain.

At the core of consciousness there is something much more profound than thought or emotion. It exists wherever consciousness exists. I call this core Observing Awareness because it is what sees and experiences everything in Active Mind.

You think a thought: "I feel like taking a walk" and Observing Awareness witnesses it. That is how you know you thunked a thought!

You have a dream while sleeping, wake up and remember your dream because Observing Awareness witnessed the dream. That is why you can use memory to retrieve it.

People throughout time and in every culture have discovered what has been called "Heaven," "Spirit," "Soul," "Atman," "Self," "Buddha Nature," "The Witness," and many other names. These are all terms describing Observing Awareness.

Each tradition communicates what people can understand at the time and in the culture it is presented. After hitting its peak, the teachings begin to diminish, wane, and eventually become unhelpful and even detrimental to genuine spiritual growth in some cases.

We find ourselves in such a time right now. Our religions need to be renewed, reinvented, or they must take their place in the museums of history as relics of the past.

What I have learned from the various spiritual communities I practiced with, is the way to renewal, the way to peace both personally and globally is through personal spiritual experience. We all need to experience and know the real "me." What Jesus called "the kingdom of heaven within."

We need to stop looking outside for what can only be discovered inside. We need to discover this for ourselves and carry it into our lives. The goal is not fantastic or religious in nature. It is simple, profound, ever-present, ever-available and the epitome of natural.

Practical Application

One of the unique features you will discover as you read It's Never too Late to Do Nothing is the blending of Buddhist meditation practices such as mindfulness meditation and compassion meditation with Yogic meditation techniques such as devotion meditation and selfless service meditation. Traditionally Yoga and Buddhism are considered different schools that share some things in common but are seemingly diametrically opposed when it comes to a few key doctrines.

The ideas discussed in this book put all emphasis on practical application. This book is designed for you to gain as many practical benefits as possible from meditation and yoga. Benefits that progress your life in a holistic way towards increased happiness, calmness, improved health and relationships and an ability to be more productive without becoming stressed.

When this book refers to yoga, it is not simply referring to Hatha Yoga, the yoga that involves physical postures, but the goal of all yogas which encompasses every facet of living as you will understand as the book unfolds.

Since practical application is the goal, I find that Buddhist and Yogic meditation practices and philosophy work well together and are great supports for one another making practice easier and more complete.

CHAPTER 1

A FOX GUARDING A CHICKEN COOP

⊶⊷

Once upon a time there was an old farmer who lived in a beautiful valley filled with fields, flowers, winding stone paths, and clear streams shaded by a cool forest. He loved being so close to nature and felt like he could listen to its wisdom every day he communed with it. His pride and joy were the wonderful chickens he cared for and nurtured to insure they were happy, healthy and productive. The eggs from his chickens were known to be the best in the land.

Everything would have been perfect if it wasn't for an uninvited visitor who was interfering with the old farmer's peace and happiness. This uninvited visitor came in the form of a fox. This fox was stealing his prized chickens almost every night. Instead of the farmer being able to enjoy his beautiful life, he was forced to worry about his chickens, struggled to protect his land and lived in fear of losing his livelihood.

One day the old farmer was complaining to his neighbor about all the chickens he was losing to the local fox. The neighbor suggested paying a few eggs per night to someone willing to guard the chickens." Certainly you're losing more than a few eggs each night now," said the neighbor. The farmer thought his neighbor's suggestion made a lot of sense and he asked if his neighbor knew anyone who might be suitable for the job.

"Well," said the neighbor, "I do have a nephew who is looking for work. He recently married and his wife is expecting their first child."

The farmer was beside himself with joy. "Wonderful! Have him meet me in front of the chicken coops at four-thirty tomorrow morning, right before the sun rises and the cock crows.

Early the next morning while the night was still dark, right before the sun starts its long arc across the sky from dawn to dusk, a red-haired fellow walked out of the forest's shadows into the faint moonlight right before the farmer's chicken coops.

His clothes were tailored from the finest materials. His hair was as thick and red as a flame under his fancy top-hat that stylishly sported a long pheasant feather tucked into its grosgrain ribbon. His suit was lined with vertical pin stripes and he smiled the most delicious smile. "I've come for the job of protecting your chickens" he said.

The old farmer said nothing. He peered at his neighbor's nephew watching every muscle in his face as the morning light ever-so-slowly started to illuminate the young man's penetrating eyes under their bushy brows.

The young man gazed back into the old farmer's face showing no lack of confidence, smiling, perfectly at ease. He stood with his arms crossing one another, calm, commanding and intelligent.

The young man told the farmer all about his accomplishments and why he was the perfect person for the job.

A sliver of morning light crept over the horizon. Its filtered brightness surrounded the chicken coops with a dull hue.

Suddenly, an old hen started clucking loudly and in a few minutes one hundred hens joined her in an uproarious noise that penetrated the valley surrounding the old farmer's land. Soon every hen in the old farmer's coops was cackling loudly!

The old man smiled broad and wide! He was beaming as he gazed into the young applicant's eyes.

Slowly, almost in-perceptively, the old farmer started to chuckle until his chuckle turned into a full belly laugh. As he roared in laughter he said, "If my hens warn each other before a cock crows at sunrise then a fox is surely near! You, who has come to guard my chicken coop is the thief in the night I've been trying to catch!"

The fox threw off his hat and as his two large ears sprung loose and his fluffy red tail came out from under his suit-coat, he asked, "Pray tell me farmer, why are you laughing then? You have spent many hours worrying your old white head about how to catch me and now that I am here, right in front of you, all you can do is laugh! Why?"

The fox was incredulous and outraged! Although he was no stranger to danger and had nearly lost his life on more than one occasion, the humiliation of hearing the old farmer's laughter at him was too much for his fragile pride. He preferred death!

"I am laughing," said the old farmer, "because I would have thought to catch a sly young fellow such as yourself, an old man like me would have to use all his strength, a library worth of knowledge, and at least ten hunters! But all I had to do was nothing!" The old man started laughing again even louder than before!

Embarrassed and ashamed, the young fox ran back into the forest hiding from the ever-growing morning light which exposed the wooded garden with its tall monumental trees, beautiful flowering bushes, cool streams and paths. The cock crowed, birds sang, and the sly fox was never seen again in the farmer's town.

CHAPTER 2
ANCIENT WISDOM

O nce in a while a book comes along that has the ability to change lives. This is one of those books. The information and the techniques you will be learning are thousands of years old and they have been used by millions of people over the past five thousand years.

Few of us living in the Western Hemisphere ever learned any of the information I am about to share with you while we were growing up. And although yoga and meditation are popular, very few people practicing either of these techniques ever learn the central teachings.

Even in the countries where these practices originated, meditation and yoga have either become unimportant in the lives of young people or they have become popularized as products. Again, like in the West, the essential teachings are missing.

Today, we need to learn and properly understand these ancient practices more than ever because they offer us something that is unavailable anywhere else in our world.

The core teachings of yoga and meditation offer us insight into the human mind: what it is, how it works, and how to use it to improve our lives and the lives of others. But unlike any model of psychology existing today, everything we learn from meditation and yoga is personally verifiable. There are no theories to believe. There is no dogma to accept. We learn and experience everything for ourselves.

In many ways yoga and meditation have been mislabeled. They are generally considered "spiritual" or "religious" philosophies and practices but they are secular in nature; more like the arts of cooking or archery. I refer to them as "spiritual practices" in this book for the sake of consistency. But as you will see for yourself, there is nothing to accept on faith and all the benefits derived are practical. These spiritual practices are also universal. Anyone can practice them from the devout to those who embrace atheism.

Meditation and yoga (I use these terms interchangeably in this book and will explain why later) improve every area of your life that involves using your mind. If you have to engage your mind to do it, meditation and yoga will show you how to do it better, easier, with greater results.

My intention in writing this book is to make the essential teachings understandable, simple, and applicable to your life. I will follow a traditional approach: first sharing knowledge and then teaching practices that will help you personally verify the knowledge you have learned. This is a classic approach to teaching meditation and yoga.

The Source

Everything discussed in this book is about your mind, how it exists and how it works. All the ideas described are either from classic Yogic, Buddhist, or Taoist sources because all three of these traditions emphasize meditation and its insights.

I combine the teachings when it seems appropriate to make them clearer, simpler, and easier to put into practice. I do not represent any particular school and have not invented anything. The bottom-line is practical application; this is my top priority.

According to the different schools of yoga and meditation, our minds are the essence of life and all activity. Everything exists through our mind. Our entire experience of life and death takes place in our mind. Even when we are interacting with other people or the world in some way, we do it through our mind. You might say our mind is a filter through which everything is known and experienced.

Most of us spend our entire life trying to better understand the world and how it works to improve our lifestyle. We go to school, we read, we try to build a career, we start a family, we create our own business, all to live a better life so we can be happier. Our entire focus is on the world outside of our own mind and body.

But wouldn't life be easier, more efficient, if we also learned how the one tool essential to our success operates? How important is a powerful telescope when we are looking at the moon through it? It is central. If our telescope isn't calibrated correctly our image will be inaccurate. Our mind is the telescope through which we view life and therefore it is the most important factor of success, happiness and health.

Our mind is made of consciousness. Our mind is consciousness. People can argue whether consciousness has an organic origin created by our brain or whether consciousness preexists our brain. But for all practical purposes - as we will see through our own experiments outlined in this book - mind is consciousness. We are conscious or aware of ourselves, others and the world. Together our conscious awareness of these three things makes up our experience of life.

The original condition of our mind, the original condition of consciousness, is best described as dimensionless and impressionless. It is empty of all qualities, like a glass of perfectly clear water that is so clear you cannot see the water without a glass around it, without light reflecting on it. I refer to this original impressionless, dimensionless consciousness as "Observing Awareness."

Observing Awareness naturally, spontaneously feels love. It is the source of our satisfaction and happiness in life and is the origin of our love, compassion and caring for others. It is why we adapt good behaviors and is the true source of morality. When we lose contact with Observing Awareness we are put into a conflictual position within ourselves. We know in our mind we should be loving and good but in our heart we don't feel loving and good.

This may be how life is for many of us but according to yoga and meditation it is not inevitable that humans are self-centered. Our limited ways of seeing others and the world simply comes about because we don't understand ourselves and we have lost contact with our own foundational experience.

Most of us, most of the time, are not aware of our original state of consciousness. We only notice the things our mind becomes conscious of. If our mind becomes aware of a beautiful ocean scene with huge blue waves pounding on white sand, we are only aware of the scene but not the Observing Awareness that sees it. We therefore take on the qualities of our ocean experience and react accordingly.

If we love ocean scenes we may feel majestic and awe inspired. We might have a creative idea or take action in a truly inspired way. If we find the ocean frightening we will internalize feelings of fear and panic. The very roar of the surf may make us want to run away. Either way, whenever we confuse our reactions for who we are, it is a mistake.

Likewise, if we read or watch something tragic in the news, we are only aware of the tragedy and the feelings it evokes in our mind. But, what if we could be aware of both the seer and the seen? What if we could be aware of our Observing Awareness and the ocean or the tragedy it sees?

We would be twice as aware and twice as intelligent as we are now. We would feel freer, more natural, spontaneous, less reactive, more loving, balanced, and consequently be more successful since our reactions would be far more creative and appropriate. We would double our ability for happiness and success and it wouldn't take any extra effort on our part.

The "fox" that we must catch is a simple error we have made in identifying who we are. We are not only our thoughts, feelings and reactions to this world, which is what most of us believe most of the time. We are also Observing Awareness, that perceives our thoughts, feelings, and reactions about this world. We are the seer and the seen. Observing Awareness is the perceiver who is untouched by anything It perceives.

The sly fox is our entrenched belief that we are only our thoughts, feelings, and reactions to life. He is blind. He has created an inner vicious circle of perceiving himself, others, and the world in the same habitual ways over and over again. With every repetition his self defeating reactions continue becoming stronger.

When we enlist our fox to make a better life for our self and for others, we are exactly like the old farmer when he became excited at the possibility of hiring his neighbor's nephew to protect his chickens.

When we understand and become aware of our mind in its original impressionless, dimensionless condition (Observing Awareness) and start comprehending ourselves as the seer as well as whatever we are seeing or experiencing, we become like the silent witnessing old farmer who simply saw through his fox.

All it takes to defeat our fox is seeing him in the light of knowledge and in the light of our firsthand experience of being the seer as well as the seen. We easily gain this ability through yoga and meditation as taught in this book.

The Path

Before we begin, we need to learn a little about the process we will be going through. We have to have some idea about the journey we are about to take.

We will be using many terms and words that can easily be misunderstood. Yoga and meditation have been incorrectly presented as religion and therefore there are literally thousands of words, phrases, and ideas about them that have misrepresented their true teachings.

For example, what "God" means in yoga and meditation has no relationship to what "God" means in Western Religion or more accurately Middle Eastern religious philosophy.

Religion is primarily a term that refers to Middle Eastern faiths that have historically spread throughout Europe, the Americas and the world. These faiths have doctrine or common belief as their central point. Whether you believe in one of these faiths or whether you consider them myths is unimportant to understanding meditation or yoga.

What's important is the awareness that common belief or doctrine is immaterial when truly understanding yoga and meditation. It's simply not what they are about. Imagining them in light of Middle Eastern faith terminology is to misunderstand them completely.

Today very few of us understand or have genuine experience with meditation and yoga. This book will help close the gap between what we think we know about yoga and meditation and what we really need to know about them, demonstrating how we can use both for a better life. After all, that was their original purpose: to make life better.

CHAPTER 3
DEFINING GOD IN YOGA AND MEDITATION

T here is an eternal infinite ever-present Spiritual Intelligence alive in our world. It is capable of guiding us, fulfilling us, and it is available to all of us every day.

It is an intelligence that opens our eyes so we can see that life is miraculous. It is an intelligence that will bring joy back into our world. It is an intelligence that will heal our relationships and bring peace to our troubled planet. This intelligence is life itself and cannot be contained or restricted in any way by anybody.

No tradition can claim it as their own. No church, temple, synagogue, or mosque can build walls around it. No nation or culture can add anything to it or take anything away from it.

Humankind's many sacred traditions are simply our collective attempts to express the same universal Spiritual Intelligence that has guided us all and made life eternally magical and livable.

As beautiful and sacred as our traditions are, they can never be the very Spiritual Intelligence that inspired them. Traditions function primarily as descriptors. All of our traditions attempt to describe the indescribable and they all come and go as culture changes. Traditions are temporary. They have the same lifecycle as everything else in nature. But the Spiritual Intelligence that inspired our world's traditions, the intelligence of life itself, has no beginning and no end. So, all of our traditions represent life but only life is life.

Although this Spiritual Intelligence exists both within and without us, it is very easy to miss. Most of us never become aware of its great compassion, power, guidance, and especially its many attempts to interact with us every day.

The old farmer in our story instinctively knew the Spiritual Intelligence that guided his life through living close to nature but he was only able to fully appreciate its presence after seeing his fox defeated with his own two eyes. Since he was familiar with Spiritual Intelligence he allowed it to solve his problem. He let life do the work for him.

The good news is we all have the same ability as the old farmer. We can all become familiar with Spiritual Intelligence, we can learn how to access it and we can learn how to get out of its way so it can catch our fox. It will guide us to our life's purpose because life naturally fulfills life.

Spiritual Intelligence can never be described in language because it is infinite in nature. When I say that Spiritual Intelligence is infinite I am not suggesting that it is so big that it is beyond us. I am also not suggesting that it is divine. Divinity has nothing to do with infinite intelligence. When we say something is divine or holy we are speaking about a concept, an idea, which only exists in relationship to its opposite - inglorious, profane, human, worldly. It has no meaning without contrast.

But when we talk about infinite Spiritual Intelligence we are talking about something beyond ideas and concepts. Spiritual Intelligence has no opposite. It is everywhere and it is nowhere. It exists everywhere outside of us and it is simultaneously within every fiber of our existence.

Practices such as meditation and yoga put us in touch with our inherent Spiritual Intelligence. Its presence in our lives is constant but we spend so much time living in our heads, perceiving everything through our thoughts and emotions, most of us are completely unaware of its influence. We don't know it exists and we don't see its potential.

When we learn to open our awareness, like one opens the aperture of a camera, to include all of our senses, our body, mind and environment, we gain a vast, new experience of our self and the world. This is how we gain intimate awareness of Spiritual Intelligence. Spiritual Intelligence is not an idea. It is a simple human experience that grows into authentic living wisdom.

Spiritual Intelligence Poem

He has no destination but he is always where he should be.

He does as he pleases but he is always in harmony with all things.

He holds no doctrine but is truth itself.

He shines like the sun but goes unnoticed through a crowd.

When he laughs demons run away and when he cries the earth weeps with joy.

He avoids attention and status but his fame is eternal.

Look for him and you will never find him. Try to forget him and he will follow you like a shadow.

Call him Tao or any name you like: words cannot comprehend him.

The only way to know him is to become him. Lead no special life, follow no path, the way is easy and clear. Just walk straight ahead.

Life, Death and Past Impressions

Life is constantly and continuously communicating with each of us every day. It does this naturally and effortlessly. Life supports life. There is nothing that can go against it.

Death is a part of life. It is simply the other side of birth. Life includes birth and death and everything that makes the two of them possible and necessary. Death is not a punishment and it doesn't diminish life in any way.

Many people have been taught that death is a type of defeat. However, if we look into the subject of death more closely, we find it is death that makes every victory possible. Our victories in life are measured by death's grip on our lives. Our lives begin and end at specific moments; birth and death together produce the framework in which we accomplish everything.

Ask yourself and answer honestly from your heart: "Is it likely that life, as miraculous and implausible as it is, made a mistake when it created birth and death?"

Another question to ask yourself: "Is it true that we created death by our sins as so many of us were taught as children? Is death really related to sin?" Isn't it much more likely that such an idea is simply some people's impression of death?

Death is here to stay and for good reason. It isn't any more possible to have birth without death than it is to have *left* without *right*, *up* without *down*, or *north* without *south*.

The first thing we must do to start recognizing Spiritual Intelligence in our lives is to let go of our assumptions about ourselves, others and life itself. A good place to start is to contemplate death: what death means to us as individuals, what it means to us as a species and ultimately what it means to us as one small planet in an infinite universe.

Our assumptions and past impressions act like weights holding us down. They stop us from learning new information that expands our worldview and our possibilities in life.

Life is ever-new and it is always fresh. Our job is to keep expanding with it. Our job is to keep refreshing our minds, bodies and spirits. It is not our job to defend, protect or continue old perspectives that have been outgrown by ourselves and others.

Traditions are wonderful connections between people over many generations. Their purposes and their functions are sacred. They are gifts from our past that we willfully extend into our future for ourselves and for others.

But traditions are meant to extend and to expand as human consciousness extends and expands. It is we who give our traditions life and they exist, ultimately, in our service. We owe them our integrity and they owe us their rich ever-new wisdom. True wisdom is always applicable anytime and in every situation.

Whenever traditions start to rule over humanity it is time to amend or abandon them. Traditions are formations left by the waves of time on the beach of life. They naturally change with the tides and the seasons. If they grow too rigid the entire environment will conspire together to end them completely and they will be washed out into the sea forever.

God in Yoga and Meditation

God is an idea we have created to describe and explain life to ourselves. Because life is essentially infinite which is verifiable through our experience of our own consciousness, there are many versions of God.

Some people think that God is separate from life and the world. If that is true then God must be limited, for how could an infinite God be *here* but not *there*? What materials would an infinite God have outside of Himself or Herself to create a universe?

The word "God" represents life in the same way the word "water" represents wet stuff. We cannot quench our thirst by thinking the word "water" and we cannot know life by understanding and believing one of the many traditional schools of thought about God.

If we want to know God, life, the infinite, we must let go of what we think we know. No one can know God because every idea we have about God is finite and limited. It is like trying to contain an ocean in a cup.

We must open up and invite God, the one Spiritual Intelligence, into our lives without fixed ideas. We must recognize that everything we believe we know about God and ourselves is more limited and problematic than we understand.

Even the boundaries we think define our very existence are highly questionable. For example, we identify ourselves as being our body but where does this body begin and end? Since our body cannot exist for even one moment without a sun, is our solar system's sun part of our body? Our human edges blur with a few simple questions.

Others identify themselves as being a soul. Although the idea of being a soul may help us imagine our existence beyond our body, it doesn't help us know who we are. Physics has explained how we physically exist beyond the boundaries of our skin but what does the idea of a soul tell us about who we are? What is a soul beyond our thoughts and feelings that constantly change? What is a self without location and circumference?

Neither of the ideas, of being a physical body or a soul, really offer us much when it comes to understanding what we are or what our purpose might be. Both are equally unhelpful when it comes to finding lasting fulfillment.

Opening up to God, Spiritual Intelligence, takes deeply asking these essential questions and then letting go. Our human mind simply is incapable of comprehending its own existence, its own purpose and strangely enough even it's own fulfillment.

The essential questions about life that need to be sincerely asked do not require answers that lead to a concrete philosophy. It is the questions themselves that open our awareness to Spiritual

Intelligence. Far too often our answers only reinforce our habitual assumptions. The very ones that hold us back from learning new insights. But simply by inviting or by allowing the possibility of connecting with a deeper reality, we begin to get out of our own way and Spiritual Intelligence becomes active in our lives.

Information, which plays such a huge part in our society is invaluable but it is irrelevant when it comes to Spiritual Intelligence. Information is a part of our past. Spiritual Intelligence is always new, always fresh, always now.

In this book, whenever I use the word "God" I am referring to Spiritual Intelligence and nothing else. The same thing is meant whenever I use the terms *life, Spiritual Intelligence, Tao, true self, true existence,* or when God is described as the union of "*the seer and the seen,*" or the union of "*form and formlessness,*" or as a "*balance between Active Mind and Observing Awareness,*" or as "*Meditation Awareness*" or the "*spiritual heart*".

God is the life force in all of us. God is everything that is alive and God is life itself. God is the individual and God is everything. God is transcendental and God is imminent, right before us.

CHAPTER 4
ENLIGHTENMENT

⊷⊶

The goal of meditation and yoga is enlightenment. In many ways the word "enlightenment" is similar to the word "God" in yoga and meditation. There is no equivalent idea in the English language. In Western History enlightenment refers to The Age of Reason, a historical period when intelligent men and women began expressing, sharing, and scientifically verifying new speculations outside church doctrine.

At that point in Western History, the Christian Church dictated everything by law enforced by the nearest emperor or monarch. In such an age, reason must have seemed enlightening. Being able to publicly "reason" without execution got this period in Western history coined The Age of Reason.

In this book, when I discuss enlightenment, I am not referring to reason or scientific process, which are both worthy pursuits. I am referring to a completely different animal. I define enlightenment as *refined human experience*. Particularly, human experience that simultaneously clarifies and expresses the essential nature of all human beings and the essential nature we share with all life forms. Enlightenment is the experience of things as they are for all of us for all time. Enlightenment can never be captured in words and turned into dogma.

According to yoga and meditation, enlightenment can be known, experienced, and expressed by anyone. It is not a rare attainment reserved for a few. Enlightenment is our nature, which is why we can experience and express it.

In this book, enlightenment is described as a balance between impressionless, dimensionless Observing Awareness, which is our original condition of consciousness, and Active Mind. I will go into detail about this experience in future chapters but what is important now is understanding when our minds and bodies are coordinated and in balance with one another, we experience and express enlightenment.

When our minds and bodies are coordinated, we are in balance with, and harmoniously relate to, every sight, sound, taste, sensation and smell that we experience through our five senses, as well as all our thoughts and emotions that we know through mind. We experience and express enlightenment spontaneously.

It's not as far fetched as it may seem. We are life. We are expressions of life. If life were an apple tree we would be its apples. If life were an ocean we would be its waves. Apples are the tree. Waves are the ocean.

It is only our thoughts about ourselves, others, and life, that make it appear that we are different from life. It seems as if "we" are living life. But actually, life is "us" like the ocean and its waves are one. It is not we but life that is living life.

Once we understand that we are inherently the same as life, we can also imagine that our conscious awareness of being life must exist within a range depending on our ability for refined human experience, which is developed through spiritual practices such as meditation. For the sake of convenience I have mapped out this range of refined experience on a scale from one to ten.

At ten, we are completely lost. We see ourselves as solid concrete individuals fighting against others and a hostile environment for survival and pleasure.

At five, we still see ourselves as concrete entities but we are well groomed, well integrated social animals with predictable lives.

At three, we start becoming aware of alternate versions of reality while keeping our feet solidly on the ground. These alternate versions of reality have nothing in common with mental illness. Meditation Awareness increases both individuality and integration with society while mental illness has chaotic influences.

At two, we begin spiritual practices and lifestyle choices that fine tune our experience of life and deepen our awareness of our own fundamental mind.

At one, we experience perfect refined human experience: our own physical, sensual, mental, emotional, harmony and balance within ourselves, with others, the world, and with life.

This balance in our awareness, perception, behavior and in our social exchanges is enlightenment. It is pure refined experience on one end and it is perfect spontaneous action on the other. It is life itself following its natural course to perfection, total autonomy and total integration.

No one can predict how an enlightened person is going to live. No one can tell you what he or she will specifically do in any area of life. Enlightenment isn't like a club we join where we accept a tradition of club house rules.

Enlightenment is something we must all experience for ourselves and something we express in our own unique way. It isn't really possible to define specific qualities or traits of an enlightened person.

But, we can get an idea of what to expect if we begin a serious spiritual practice of meditation and yoga. The following four qualities are all signs of growing enlightened mind and are also symptoms of enlightened mind. They are not spiritual practices but they are the natural outcomes of the spiritual practices of meditation and yoga.

This last point is important. It will serve no purpose to *practice* the following four qualities of enlightened mind, turning them into spiritual practices. You will not be able to attain any of them through personal effort.

The practices of meditation and yoga taught in this book develop into these qualities of enlightened mind exactly as an apple seed develops into an apple. You cannot will them into existence on your own.

Openness

Openness is not an act of will. You cannot choose to open. If you choose openness it is not openness. This is always the case.

At some point in our spiritual evolution we all open. We open exactly like a flower opens, but as human beings our petals are seeing, hearing, smelling, tasting, feeling and our mind's awareness. Mental awareness includes our thoughts, emotions, Perceptual Awareness and dreams.

Tuning into our five senses and our mind's awareness cultivates openness. This requires letting go and being fully present in the moment. We don't try to let go, we just let go. Likewise, we don't try to be fully in the present, we are the present.

When we open we are suddenly aware of it all, at once, everything entering our awareness through our senses and our mind, harmoniously working together within our field of perception. It is all one field and it is all separate objects of awareness, all at the same time. This is openness.

To get a clearer understanding of openness it is helpful to grasp its opposite which is dogma. When we choose to accept dogma we choose to passionately believe an idea or an interpretation of life, and the entire process takes place on the thinking emotional level of our mind.

It is a choice, an act of will. Our choices, and likewise our acts of will in life, are always colored by our past experiences, impressions, fixed ideas and bias. Choices are products of our past. Openness is always out of the now. Openness expands our sensual and mental awareness while being preoccupied with our mental world in the forms of our beliefs and memories shuts them down.

Living in the now doesn't mean nature or life is chaotic. Natural laws do exist but they are natural laws and therefore they are never fixed or "written in stone."

Natural laws cannot be written down or memorized. They are always operational and changing. They can be observed in limited ways but they are infinitely applicable, infinitely adaptable, and they express themselves in unique ways depending on the people and the situations involved. Ways that cannot be anticipated and sometimes go unseen.

How can you tell dogma from natural law? Simple. Test them. Dogma is static and natural law is dynamic. You can know dogma but you can only spontaneously live natural law and openness.

Honesty

Honesty is an extension of our openness. It is simply being open from the inside. In openness, we expanded our inner awareness to include everything inside and outside.

In honesty, we extend our inner experience of openness to the outer world. We are inviting everything and everyone to benefit from our openness. It is the greatest contribution we can ever make because it equally includes the individual and the whole. Honesty is sincere and even childlike in its loving feeling. Everyone relaxes around a truly honest person.

Honesty is naturally humble. Humility is simply respect for others. We are all spontaneously humble whenever our hearts recognize the immensity of life. Living honestly increases the likelihood that we will recognize the immensity of life.

Honesty is unbelievably efficient when compared to other life strategies because living honestly will offer us life's lessons as soon as they become available. A good start is simply being open about our mistakes, being willing to admit an error and change our perspective and behavior as soon as our error becomes obvious.

This is one way our openness can start expressing itself through us as genuine honesty. Genuine honesty is much more than speaking the truth. It is feeling and understanding the integrity of life. Authentic openness always manifests as genuine honesty.

In genuine honesty we don't identify with any of our successes or our failures. It is all coming through us because we are channeling Spiritual Intelligence. We take responsibility but not ownership. With this attitude we are always willing to learn and we never become defensive or guarded.

Dharma

There is no equivalent term for "dharma" anywhere outside of India. Although the concept of dharma spread with Buddhism, Hinduism and Yoga throughout Asia, Europe, America, and eventually the whole world, the definition of Dharma originated in India and its definition is Indian. Dharma is a Sanskrit word.

It is sometimes translated as "eternal way." Other times it is translated as "one's duty" and at other times still it is translated "things as they are." In this book, I use the term "dharma" all three ways because these three definitions are actually three different levels of the same reality.

When discussing Spiritual Intelligence, dharma is referred to as the "eternal way": life follows a natural eternal process that starts from a state of total equilibrium and unity, completely unaware of itself.

Within life there arises a spontaneous desire to know itself. There is an energetic event, an explosion of sorts, that infinitely expands and infinitely contracts at the same time.

Life moves into a dysregulated condition, manifesting infinite life forms with varying degrees of awareness and forgetfulness.

Life completes the cycle as each of these infinite life forms recognizes its original state of equilibrium and union. This process is the "eternal way." This is dharma.

When we talk about dharma related to finding our life's purpose, we are talking about what we do naturally to benefit ourselves and others. All of us have a particular talent that needs to be expressed in society. It is our personal contribution to the world, our life's purpose. These inclinations that express our nature and improve our life and the life of others are known as dharma. Everything in nature has a dharma. The sun's dharma is to shine, water's dharma is to nourish all life, just as Spiritual Intelligence has its dharma on a universal level.

Dharma also exists on an experiential level when we experience the world as it truly is. Usually we experience everything through our own perceptual filter. Our filter is made out of our personal bias' based on our former experiences. We develop a certain way of seeing everything in life based on our past impressions and these impressions develop into habits. We perceive something a given way and we react to it accordingly.

These patterns become limiting and they block us from fulfilling our potential. When we experience ourselves, others, and the world without our past impressions we are literally seeing dharma, literally being dharma. We see things as they are and seeing reality makes our path in life crystal clear. The experience of dharma grows out of our experience of openness and authentic honesty, and it naturally grows into inner integrity.

Trust

Trust is different from faith. "Faith," as we commonly use the word today, refers to belief. Belief in an idea or a thought. "I believe there is life after death" is a popular belief. Trust is unrelated to belief. We learn to float in water by trusting. The act of floating requires letting go, the act of believing is more like hanging on to a rock. They are very different from one another.

Trust is a result of experiencing and knowing inner integrity. Whatever we feel inside we see outside. When we know how to experience our own consciousness, our own mind, without it being colored by our past impressions, we realize the center of our being is the same as the center of everything. This leads to feeling deep love. This is trust. We let go into life through self knowledge.

Trust is also a pivotal point in our spiritual evolution. Trust empowers our experience of openness which verifies and strengthens the entire process of Openness, Honesty, Dharma and Trust, making it a new way of living. It is the crucial point where self transformation takes place. This is where our life actually changes from a limited condition into a much more expanded condition.

To describe how these four qualities work together, here is a synopsis: Opening to our own full panoramic awareness of our senses and our mental awareness allows us to see things as they are. Honesty allows us to share things as they are and dharma puts our life in balance with things as they are. Once our lives are in balance we discover inner integrity that grows into trust.

CHAPTER 5
SPIRITUAL INTELLIGENCE

O ne of the most powerful natural tools to tap into Spiritual
Intelligence is our own perception or how we see things.
Every one of us has our own unique worldview. Our worldview may
share things in common with the world views of others but if we
look closely and are honest with ourselves, we will see that each
of us sees ourselves, others, the world, and life in our own unique
way.

Even if we belong to the same religion, political party, or lifestyle
as someone, if we really sit down with that person and compare our
interpretations of our common faith, party, or way of living, we will
recognize differences.

This can be very threatening to some of us who rely on sharing
common bonds with others as a means to personal security, a sense
of who we are and our purpose in life. But if we are able to shift our
perception and realize our self beyond group security the experience
will be liberating.

All religions and spiritual paths alter our worldview. By offering us a particular perspective on life they change our daily experience. We can change our personal worldview and our experience very much like we change television stations with our TV remote.

We may feel like our worldview is the same thing as our self and therefore it is impossible to change, but it isn't true. Our feelings of resistance are created by our *identification* with our worldview.

We have ingrained our worldview into our mind so deeply that it has become interwoven throughout our personality, like thread throughout a winter coat. They seem to be one and the same thing but they are not the same thing.

Our self is not a worldview. All of us once were infants. We were perfectly alive and perfectly ourselves without any worldview. Our self puts on a worldview much like we put on a hat and just like a hat after a while we forget we have it on!

The more we recognize that our personal perspective of life is porous and changeable the more we start realizing that our true self is formless. I refer to this formless self as the "seer" or "Observing Awareness" and all the forms it sees and becomes identified with are referred to as the "seen" or as parts of "Active Mind."

Our self cannot be nailed down or defined in any way. This is why it was referred to as "spirit" in some religious communities. Spirituality teaches us that our true self, who and what we really are, exists beyond anything in form, or in other words anything we experience through our five senses, think, believe, imagine, feel, do or understand. Spiritual practices are methods that foster our direct experience of our true self. I refer to the experience of true self in this book as Meditation Awareness.

I would like you to explore Spiritual Intelligence through using your own power of perception. Spiritual Intelligence is a tricky thing to understand at first because it is not an idea to believe or a concept. It is a living process that is always active in our lives whether we recognize it or not.

Exploring and contemplating Spiritual Intelligence as suggested below, will assist you in starting the process of seeing beyond your longstanding assumptions about yourself and life. As your assumptions are recognized as impressions from your past experiences, Spiritual Intelligence will become more obviously active in your life.

I offer you a mental exercise in this chapter that I encourage you to "try on" like a new hat. It is a spiritual practice. It doesn't make any difference whether you believe what I am sharing or not. You can even dislike the whole idea. But if you intentionally practice contemplating Spiritual Intelligence you will learn how to change your daily experience and you will be on your way to learning who and what your true self is.

Read the rest of this chapter in its entirety and then start practicing seeing yourself, others, the world, and life through the eyes of Spiritual Intelligence. Remember, practicing seeing the world, others and yourself through the *idea* of Spiritual Intelligence is not the same thing as Spiritual Intelligence. Spiritual Intelligence is spontaneous. There is no way to control Spiritual Intelligence through personal effort. However, contemplating Spiritual Intelligence prepares the ground for understanding your experiences during meditation and yoga practices which activate Spiritual Intelligence in your life.

Simply contemplate and read about Spiritual Intelligence repeatedly and practice intentionally seeing the world through its eyes.

Remember: the point of this practice is to recognize your assumptions or past impressions so that you can see beyond them and to assist you in recognizing Spiritual Intelligence in your life. I am not asking you to believe or disbelieve anything. Belief systems are irrelevant to spiritual practice.

It might be a good idea to write notes on the changes you observe in your daily experience that come from contemplating Spiritual Intelligence.

The point of this practice is not to convince you of accepting a new worldview. There are plenty of people in your life who are already doing that.

The point of this practice is to increase your awareness of the process of creating any worldview and all world views. This exercise will teach you how you plant things into your own mind. The process is enlightening.

The spiritual practices offered throughout this book will assist you in contemplating and recognizing Spiritual Intelligence in your life. All the practices have the same goal: all of them activate and support your awareness of Spiritual Intelligence.

Spiritual Intelligence Contemplation: Part I

Everything that happens in life and in the world at large is exactly what is supposed to happen. It is exactly what must happen. We may believe that we are in control of our life and that we know what should happen, but there is a grander scheme to life than our personal world and that grander scheme includes everything and everybody for all time.

It is not possible for most of us to have a worldview that includes everything and everyone for all time and consequently our personal perspective or beliefs about life are limiting.

Some people have the spiritual practice of having a worldview that includes everything and everybody for all time, but life in its entirety, already has such a perspective because of its own infinite nature and infinite self-awareness.

Life can be divided into two interactive parts: form or infinite nature and formlessness or infinite self-awareness. The formless is constant and all forms are impermanent.

Everything that exists comes out of the formless and when its existence has ended it goes back into the formless.

Another way of describing this process is that the formless manifests as all forms and at the end of each form's life it returns to its original state of formlessness.

There is no such thing as form without formlessness and there is no such thing as formlessness without form. They are two sides of the same coin. Life represents form and death represents formlessness.

If an individual form, whatever it may be, is in balance with the formless then that individual form is aware of both its form and its formless center.

When realized together they create a genuine experience of true self or Tao, which is the same experience as becoming one with God through love. I call this realization Meditation Awareness.

If the individual form is out of balance with the formless then it remains unaware of its formless center.

If we experience Meditation Awareness, which is formlessness and form together, then all of our thoughts, emotions, words and actions are perfectly aligned with the infinite universe which is the sum of infinite forms and infinite formlessness.

If we are unaware of our own formless center and we believe we are simply our form (our body, our thoughts, our emotions, our words, and our behaviors), then our experience of life will be isolated and limited and we will be out of balance with the infinite universe. Life is infinite by nature and its nature is realized and actualized through our human experience and expression of it.

One of the symptoms of being out of balance with the universe is feeling chronically stressed. A feeling that something is wrong either with ourselves or the world at large. Life just doesn't seem right to us. We complain about how things are and we are convinced that if everybody listened to us and shared our perspective that life would be better.

We are only aware of the forms of the universe and we therefore see forms as competing with one another. Whose form is going to be the dominant? We see this perspective in the media every day in many different areas of society such as in the economy, politics and religion.

Whose religion is correct? Whose economic plan will win? Which political party has the most power? From this perspective life is very uncomfortable, stressful and limiting. There literally is no peace. It is a world of endless conflict.

But when we are aware of both form and formlessness (Meditation Awareness) everything in our world comes together. This is because only formlessness can expose how all of life's infinite forms exist harmoniously.

I described this way of being alive, this way of living, in Chapter Four as *Openness, Honesty, Dharma* and *Trust*. We live in harmony with our life's purpose no matter what is going on around us or in the world at large.

God is another word for life. When we know God, our self, as we truly exist, we know life. Our experience of our life becomes crystal clear, refined, and it enriches everyone else's experience of their life.

The infinite universe is always in perfect balance. Even when things get knocked off balance and appear to be awful or even horrible from our perspective, such as when there are wars or we have to survive an epidemic, the universe is still in perfect balance.

From worldwide horrors, all the way to minor body aches, every form of suffering is an imbalance in our awareness of the universal relationship between form and the formless. Or you can equally see everything that happens in life as being one big imbalance in the infinite universe's awareness of its own infinite forms and its own infinite self-awareness.

Life is always perfect. Even imbalance is a part of infinite balance. Life cannot defeat itself. The worst imaginable conditions of chaos, destruction and death, individually and globally, all exist because of their common states of imbalance. But they are all temporary fluctuations taking place within the infinite forms of an infinite universe all grounded in infinite formlessness. Nothing can touch our formless center, our true self. Nothing. Knowing and experiencing this is the goal of spiritual life.

Of course from our usual perspective life isn't perfect. Very few of us know our formless center. Our feelings about how things should *be* rub up against what *is* every day. This is one of our core conflicts no matter who we are.

There is life on one hand, that is too vast to comprehend, stretching forever into the past and into the future. And then there is us, with our narrow, constricted, understanding, comprehension, and limited experiences of life.

Many of us have set out to master life not understanding that all true masters of life have completely surrendered to life. By "surrender" I mean they have balanced their own personal wills with a personal awareness of formlessness discovered through spiritual practices. For them, life is balanced and they naturally feel love, compassion, joy, and humor. They live life fully alive and they do not begrudge their death nor do they consider it a dishonor.

All of life is perfect exactly as it is.

Spiritual Intelligence Contemplation: Part II

The second part of Spiritual Intelligence is the truth of spiritual evolution. Every form in existence is slowly evolving towards realization of the formless as its center.

The more of us who accomplish spiritual evolution the easier it will be for others to evolve. Consequently, the less of us who have spiritually evolved the harder it will be for anyone to evolve. This law of the infinite universe is an expression of the universe interacting within itself.

Everything we do, everything we experience, everything that happens to us, are all expressions of the one Spiritual Intelligence.

As we begin to realize life's essential quality of unity inside and out, we loosen our grip on life. We stop our endless attempts to manipulate it. We can let go a little and trust.

Life is still gonna hurt sometimes but we can learn to let the hurts go as soon as they stop hurting and we don't have to spend our time anticipating the next pain.

If we explore situations or relationships that we cannot accept as perfect we will learn what causes us to judge life, causing us much unnecessary pain. It is always our thoughts about life and what we think should and should not happen.

But if we investigate what our thinking mind is, we learn that it is only one aspect of human awareness. It is like looking through a window into a beautiful field of flowers mistaking the view for the field itself.

Our thoughts about life are not life. They are a view of life. Yet we give them power over our whole life.

As we evolve we will experience ourselves in radically new ways. We will become aware of formlessness, an actual part of our self that exists beyond our thinking mind and yet is the essence of our mind.

First, we will experience it inside ourselves as our core center and then outside in others as their core center simultaneously.

As our awareness grows, we will reach a balance between experiencing ourselves as form and experiencing ourselves as formlessness. This shift in our perspective, which I call Meditation Awareness, will spontaneously ripple out into our experience of the world revealing to us that everything in life is truly perfect exactly as it is.

Our new experience of life will make us exceptionally skill-ful in everyday practical living by increasing our creativity, prob-lem solving abilities, relationship skills, and feelings of love and compassion.

In order to clarify how form and formlessness manifest in dif-ferent ways depending on our circumstances, here are two common examples:

When experiencing form and formlessness in our behavior we can call them *doing* and *being*. We may be totally engaged in athletic activity but during our activity we feel being or stillness.

For example, while jogging we feel as if we are doing nothing. It is as if jogging is going on by itself and we are merely a witness along for the ride. In this example, doing is form and being is formlessness.

If we are discussing a musical composition and we want to un-derstand it in terms of form and formlessness, we would perceive the music as a relationship between sound and silence. Sound is form and silence is formlessness.

We discover that sound is actually silence vibrating. We usually only notice the music or the sounds we are hearing but if we are really mindful we will notice that silence is the common thread running between all notes or sounds. Silence is the one constant. It is formless-ness and the sounds we hear are the forms it creates.

Here are a few exercises that will help you start contemplating and exploring Spiritual Intelligence:

1. Start out each morning, as you are preparing for your day, re-minding yourself everything that happens today is an expression

of a perfect infinite universe that knows exactly what it is doing. This doesn't mean that you cannot feel sad about someone's loss or that you shouldn't get angry about injustice. You don't need to change your emotional responses. Simply remind yourself that although from your limited view things may seem wrong, they are all perfect expressions of Spiritual Intelligence. Things are only wrong on a relative level of life. On an absolute level of life, everything is always perfect.

2. Feel your breath throughout the day. Feel your exhalations as they pass through your nostrils. Feel the pause at the end of each exhalation right before you start your next inhalation. If you practice this simple exercise you will start to feel some space between you and your thoughts as well as your emotions. You will still think the same thoughts and feel your usual feelings but they will not be able to grab you and make you buy into them as if they are ultimate reality. This "space" is an experience of formlessness.

3. Listen to the silence in between the sounds you hear, whether it is listening to music, hearing someone speak, cars going by, a bird singing, machinery, etc. The silence will always be there in between the sounds you perceive. This will expand your awareness of formlessness and enhance your ability to listen.

4. As you visually perceive your world, look at the spaces between the forms you see. A winter tree is a good example. Look at the space between the branches along with the form of the tree. See how the entire image of form and formless, tree and space, completes the visual experience of the tree as well as every other object you see.

5. As you go through your day notice the relationship between form and formlessness in action and stillness no matter what you are

doing. We do not perform actions like we think we do. Every action we perform consists of movement and stillness that includes a pause exactly like the pause we discovered between our breaths. We lift a cup of water to our mouth and our arm and hand pause as they touch the cup. Our arm moves again as we lift the cup to our mouths and then pauses again when the cup touches our lips. All action is a dance between movement and stillness.

6. Read this chapter many times to make certain you understand every nuance and angle of Spiritual Intelligence. The more you become familiar with the ideas expressed the more you will be able to see them in action in your life.

7. Start a journal or take notes describing any changes you notice in your experience of daily life. Explain why you think these changes are taking place and how they are related to your practice of exploring Spiritual Intelligence.

8. Try to identify and understand the process of absorbing a new worldview and reflect on other world views that you have or have had throughout your life.

9. Deeply sincerely ask yourself: if I am not my worldview what am I? Recognize that absolutely everything that you believe makes up "you" is impermanent except for your formless center or as we also call it, "Observing Awareness."

CHAPTER 6

MEDITATION

⊯ ⊰

One of the key practices for experiencing Spiritual Intelligence is mindfulness meditation. This chapter is devoted to understanding and describing the meditation experience. It will also teach you how to verify that your meditation experience is accurate and authentic.

Most mindfulness teachers shy away from describing meditation experience. Many people these days learn mindfulness meditation during a series of half-day to one day workshops that typically run one or two days. These workshops are often taught by physicians or mental health professionals. Others learn meditation from books, blogs or YouTube videos.

No matter how people learn, most sincerely try to practice. But while they are practicing they find themselves wondering: "Am I doing this right?", "How do I know I am meditating?", or "How will I know if this is working?"

They are like people hiking through a jungle without a guide or a compass. Without intimate communication between themselves and someone who can answer their questions and point out landmark insights most will miss many significant lessons along the way and some will eventually give up.

Mindfulness meditation is an art and as with any art, technique is only one piece of the whole picture. We need to become completely familiar with our practice in the same everyday fashion an artisan baker is familiar with the entire process of baking. He or she knows every nuance.

Traditionally, Buddhist teachers who have kept the practice of mindfulness meditation alive for thousands of years have avoided descriptions of meditation experience and looked upon them with suspicion - often for good reason.

The simple truth is no one can accurately describe meditation experience because the experience is so foundational to human consciousness that it would be like our eyes trying to see themselves or our ears trying to hear themselves. It simply cannot be done.

However, considering our current cultural climate, where many of us spend much of our time simply trying to keep up with the demands of our life - withstanding stress and conflict in our personal lives and at work - we must try to do the impossible and find a way to communicate about meditation experience. This is because meditation experience offers a unique solution to our personal, interpersonal and social stress.

Meditation does not simply sedate tension like medication or express it like exercise, which both bring only temporary relief and offer no insight into its causes.

Meditation unwinds tension at its inner roots, in our thinking emotional mind, where we habitually unconsciously create it day after day. With meditation we do not need theories about stress and conflict because we observe them directly.

Today, most of us learning meditation are unfamiliar with the cultures where the technique was developed and practiced for thousands of years. People of cultures such as India, Tibet, China and Japan, not very long ago, grew up learning and imbibing the myths, rituals and teachings about the practice and goal of meditation. For them understanding the meditation experience was intuitive.

We come from a different culture with its own history. We need our own understanding about what we are supposed to experience during meditation because there is literally no equivalent for meditation experience in our current or past cultural references and lifestyles.

It is impractical at this point in meditation's cultural transition into Western culture, to teach meditation without discussing such an essential question about the practice as: "How do I know I am meditating correctly?"

I have learned from my own practice, that each student needs to discover his or her "Inner Posture," an internal experiential method for confirming they are meditating correctly.

When we are in the zone of meditation experience, when it is happening naturally and spontaneously, there is a real sense of Inner Posture that we know and feel.

Our spine is effortlessly straight. Our breathing is naturally deep. Our senses are fully open. Our radius of awareness has no edges. Our mind is free to think and feel and we intuitively gain an awareness of a sense of wakefulness running through every fiber of our self and our experience of the moment.

This is Inner Posture.

We do not need to check our Inner Posture because if we did we would be distracting ourselves from practicing the technique of meditation. Rather, we will spontaneously notice our Inner Posture when we meditate naturally and effortlessly.

Although on one hand, there are no correct or incorrect experiences during meditation, on the other hand we all do share a general meditation experience.

Traditionally, a person would learn meditation from a teacher or master, and become his or her apprentice. Teachers would guide each student's understanding of their personal meditation experiences and through this process a student would become familiar with the goal of meditation.

In time, a student would become grounded in his or her own sense of Inner Posture as their teacher helped them discover and clarify it. Once grounded in Inner Posture, the meditation experience itself would further guide the student to complete familiarity with both the practice and its goal.

Such apprenticeships are very rare these days for a variety of reasons. So we must do the best we can to help one another through the written and spoken word, even if our attempts are clumsy and imperfect.

To help facilitate this process, I created a "meditation map" that describes the basics of what a person will experience when gaining a sense of Inner Posture during meditation.

The meditation map was developed as an aid to understanding fundamental experiences that occur during meditation and to be used as a source of common language to discuss meditation experience.

Meditation Map

Active Mind

Active Mind includes everything in human awareness that is transitory. Everything that comes into our mind, stays awhile and passes.

Active Mind is made up of our thoughts, emotions, all the information that comes through our five senses and our Perceptual Awareness. Perceptual Awareness organizes our sensual impressions and thoughts together so they produce our moment by moment experiences and our sense of being a separate person, a separate experiencer. This separate experiencer is what some call the "ego."

Active Mind also includes our dreams and dreamless sleep, which are both temporary states. When we are awake our sense perceptions and mind are tightly organized in Perceptual Awareness much like a conductor leading a classical orchestra and when we are dreaming our sense perceptions and mind are loosely organized in Perceptual Awareness much like a jazz band jamming.

Observing Awareness

Observing Awareness is the continuous observer of everything in Active Mind. It is also known in this book as the "seer," the "formless," the "witness" and the "self." Observing Awareness does not come and go like all the things that make up Active Mind.

It is the one constant in our endlessly changing field of consciousness. You can visualize Observing Awareness as light shining from a flashlight and Active Mind as everything it makes visible.

Observing Awareness is what *sees* or *experiences* everything in our Perceptual Awareness.

If we see an apple, our eyes perceive its shape and color, which is organized by our mind and senses. Our Perceptual Awareness of the apple is complete when it becomes a thought or word with which we label the object, "Apple." Depending on our past experiences with apples, ego will have either one of three reactions: We will desire it, ignore it or dislike it.

Observing Awareness observes the entire process with zero involvement. It simply sees and experiences "apple" from our eyes first glimpse of its shape and color all the way through our reaction.

It is also Observing Awareness that experiences our dreams at night which is why we are able to use memory to retrieve them in the morning. Our mind and senses may be dreaming but Observing Awareness is awake to watch our dreams.

Observing Awareness can be described as pure wakefulness. It is what is awake in consciousness to perceive consciousness's infinite variety of objects and experiences.

Observing Awareness is something that each meditator must experience for him or herself. It is not an article of faith or something to believe.

Ramana Maharshi, an enlightened master, described Observing Awareness or the "Self" this way: *The Self is ever there, there is nothing without it. Be the Self and the desires and doubts will disappear. Such Self is the witness in sleep, dream and waking states of existence. These states belong to the ego. The Self transcends even the ego. Did you not exist in sleep? Did you know then that you were asleep or unaware of the world? It is only in the waking state that you describe the experience of sleep as being unawareness; therefore the consciousness when asleep is the same as that when awake. If you know what this waking consciousness is, you will know the consciousness which witnesses all the three states. Such consciousness could be found by seeking the consciousness as it was in sleep[2].*

Meditation Awareness

Meditation Awareness is a unique state of awareness which is also a natural human experience that happens throughout our day, such as when we are falling asleep. Every night, we experience a few moments when we are falling asleep when we are not fully awake but we are not asleep yet either.

We experience the same few moments again when we are waking in the morning and we start becoming aware of our surroundings but we are still grounded in our internal world. These are spontaneous moments of Meditation Awareness.

When we practice meditation we learn a technique that produces Meditation Awareness on a regular basis. The main point of meditation practice is to consciously experience Meditation Awareness and to become familiar with it. We want to experience it regularly so we know and understand it through and through.

---

[2] Talks with Sri Ramana Maharshi page 15 - SRI RAMANASRAMAM Tiruvannamalai 2006. Published by V.S. Ramanan President, Board of Trustees Sri Ramanasramam Tiruvannamalai 606 603 Tamil Nadu India

During Meditation Awareness all of our five senses are open and unrestricted. We hear every sound that enters our ears; we see every sight before us in our immediate surroundings; we taste any tastes that may be present; we feel our body's sensations as we sit or walk, and we smell any aromas in the air.

We are simply aware without concentrating on anything. Concentration is similar to a camera's aperture focusing on one object excluding everything else in the environment. It is constrictive. But Meditation Awareness is like our camera's aperture fully opened. It is expansive.

During Meditation Awareness our mind thinks whatever thoughts it thinks and because our attention is open, all thoughts naturally rise and pass. This is known as "non-thinking" in the Zen tradition. We are thinking freely and spontaneously but we do not restrict our attention to any one of our thoughts. We do not engage with them. We also feel any emotions that may rise in our awareness and again we don't engage any of them.

We cannot use effort to produce non-thinking. It simply occurs as a byproduct of the meditation technique. It is not possible to "observe your thoughts" intentionally as some mindfulness teachers instruct because we already are observing our thoughts! That is how we know we are thinking. It doesn't require any extra effort.

What we want to do is become aware of the part of ourselves that is observing - what I call Observing Awareness - and that is accomplished by the mindfulness technique itself and not by any effort on our part.

With our senses wide open and our mind unrestricted we slowly become aware of our own inherent Observing Awareness.

Meditation Awareness is this combination of experiencing Active Mind and Observing Awareness together.

This is authentic meditation. This is what we need to experience, understand, and verify with other experienced meditators.

As we become familiar with Meditation Awareness we become equally aware of our Inner Posture or what it feels like when our awareness, senses, body and mind are relaxed, open and paying attention.

Meditation Awareness makes it possible for the first time in our lives to fully know ourselves. We see our psychological, physical and behavioral patterns without having an opinion about them. We simply see ourselves exactly as we are, through and through, and our awareness naturally changes the patterns we observe without any additional effort on our part.

Most of us are very limited when it comes to authentically changing ourselves even if we have mastered our behavior. It is our old fox again guarding our chicken coop. It is our mind that creates most of our problems and so we cannot expect our exerted efforts which are products of our mind to fix them.

As Albert Einstein said: "We can't solve problems by using the same kind of thinking we used when we created them."

Problems created by mind cannot be fixed by mind. They are resolved through Meditation Awareness because it is only possible to see ourselves without opinion and without judgment through Meditation Awareness. It cannot be achieved by intellectual insight or our efforts to be "nonjudgmental" with the intention of improving our lives.

What we all can do is practice the art of mindfulness meditation and learn how to allow the practice to untangle our awareness from all our ingrained psychological, physical and behavioral patterns. We can thoroughly become familiar with ourselves. Instead of struggling against our impulses, habits and personal conflicts we can learn to truly be ourselves. Spiritual Intelligence takes care of the rest.

CHAPTER 7

INNER POSTURE

—◄+ +►—

Living mindfully is a natural development that springs out of our mindfulness meditation sitting and walking practices. First we sit, then we walk, then we extend our practice into every area of life. No one helps us. We either practice and learn or we don't. It is essential that we bounce our thoughts, experiences and questions off of other people, especially experienced meditators but ultimately only personal experience of Meditation Awareness progresses us.

You will find people who will tell you that you can skip sitting mindfulness meditation but they are most likely trying to sell you something. It may or may not be a product. Sometimes people attach mindfulness meditation to all sorts of things: therapies, lifestyles, religions, philosophies and science.

Meditation is recognizing our own consciousness exactly as it is so the knowledge we gain can be applied to anything. However, this benefit is secondary to the art of meditation practice and the experience of consciousness itself.

The first step is to practice meditation, develop a relationship to our practice, and find our Inner Posture so we can experience Meditation Awareness for ourselves.

Many people have taught and written about meditation in scientific terms over the past few decades to explain its benefits in contemporary language and this has helped push meditation's acceptance into mainstream society. It has been very helpful.

The only drawback is that people have started looking at meditation practice as a technique, a form of technology, and this prevents them from becoming intimate with their own practice.

We can discuss and understand mindfulness as a technology but we must practice it as an art. For example, we can look at medication as a form of technology because our role is passive. Laboratory and processing technologies are used to produce a product from the knowledge of pharmacology. All we do is swallow a pill as prescribed and we get a result.

If we compare technology's approach to something as human and earthy as gardening, we see big differences in the approaches and personal investments necessary in these two very different processes.

In gardening "we get our hands dirty" so to speak. It requires our full participation and as anyone knows who has had the good fortune of tasting a dedicated gardener's vegetables, personal involvement and personal investment produce a far superior vegetable, fruit and flower.

We need to practice mindfulness meditation as if we were gardening, cooking, painting, creating music, shooting archery, dancing, sculpting or becoming the finest athlete. No one can become proficient at any of these arts simply by swallowing a pill or practicing a technique.

Unfortunately that is how many people practice meditation. They learn the technique, go home and practice it, and wait for the results. After a while they get tired of waiting and assume that either they have failed at meditation or that mindfulness isn't for them. They go on living their lives believing they tried meditation and it didn't work for them when actually they never got started.

Once we learn how to practice sitting mindfulness meditation we must get involved with our practice, we must "get our hands dirty." Since we are beginners we need to start off by securing the physical space where we practice. We have to begin with the "practical" part of our practice.

Having a special area or room in your apartment or house where you practice meditation is very helpful especially when you are just starting out. After practicing daily in your meditation space for some time, you will notice that your mind and body start automatically opening into Meditation Awareness when you enter your space and sit to practice. Just noticing this pattern is encouraging and a sign of progress. Your mind and body are tuning into Meditation Awareness out of habit and you are becoming familiar with your own sense of Inner Posture.

Another ritual that is very helpful is choosing a set of clothing that you only wear during meditation. Having a meditation uniform also signals your mind and body that its time to shift your attention from preoccupation with your thoughts and feelings about the outside world (other people and situations) to resting in Meditation Awareness.

You can choose whatever space and clothing you wish but a few guidelines are helpful. Your meditation space should be clean, simple, natural, clutter-free, preferably quiet and dignified.

Your meditation uniform should be clean, simple, comfortable, loose around your body and dignified. All of these qualities help bring the mind to a state of simplicity, alertness, and a feeling of being grounded. They also send a signal to your mind that it is time to meditate.

You can place anything in your meditation space that supports your practice and your life's goals. Some people prefer natural objects such as wood, flowers and stones while others prefer photographs, statues or paintings of people that represent divine or enlightened qualities such as love, compassion and wisdom. It's all good as long as it encourages your awareness of Inner Posture and supports your experience of Meditation Awareness.

Remember, we discover our Inner Posture by noticing those moments when we are effortlessly sitting upright, feeling each breath as we inhale and exhale, thinking whatever thoughts we think, with all of our senses openly sending their impressions into our consciousness, like rivers flowing into a sea.

The key is effortlessness. We want to take special notice of what our mind, body and senses are doing and how it feels when we meditate effortlessly. The inner sensation of meditating effortlessly is a unique experience. In time, it becomes our guide, teaching us how to meditate more naturally and deeply. It can also show us our habitual obstacles.

At such moments feel your state, your mind and body together. Notice the inner energy you experience. It is self-existing. It is simply present with no effort on your part to create such an experience. Notice how your mind and senses are active but you are not interpreting your world as you usually do by analyzing everything.

This is possible because you are experiencing two things at once. You are experiencing your own Perceptual Awareness, made up of your mind, your senses and their impressions, and you are also experiencing a *feeling* of observing it all rather than analyzing everything and making conclusions about it.

During such moments we are aware of both Active Mind and Observing Awareness together and we experience Meditation Awareness. Getting a feeling for this is Inner Posture. After some time Inner Posture becomes automatic.

CHAPTER 8
STAGES OF MEDITATION

※

Although there are no cut and dry stages of meditation practice sequentially leading to some fixed goal of enlightenment, there are some general common developments that happen to many of us along the way. Even a vague understanding of these developments is helpful if we recognize them in our own practice.

Nothing is Happening Stage

This is where most of us begin and where many of us never go beyond. We learn how to meditate and we start practicing with no idea of what we are supposed to experience or how to know if we are meditating correctly.

We often have a reason we started practicing such as lowering our stress or improving our concentration. We want to decrease our blood pressure or heal from a life-threatening illness. Sometimes we just want to become more productive.

We follow the directions the best we can and hope something will change or we will notice some good result. Then it dawns on us: *nothing is happening!*

There are a variety of ways people react to this stage. Some people push on and try harder. Others feel like a failure and take it personally. Some blame the practice and become defensive. Many develop obstacles to avoid meditating and feel better when they stop.

There are endless reactions people have when it dawns on them they aren't getting what they hoped for. At this point they are still treating the practice of meditation like it is a business deal: "I put in the time where is my pay check?"

Mirror Stage

If we persist in our practice despite our disappointment over not receiving any of the things we were hoping to receive, we are given a flash of recognition, an "ah-ha moment." We realize that all of our reactions to the practice of meditation are reflections of our own psychological, physical and behavioral patterns. How we meditate is how we live. But, unlike any other method of insight or reflection, there is no underlying perspective or assumption driving our insights.

There is no religious, philosophical, therapeutic or cultural wedge of interpretation between us and our personal patterns of living. Even our own perspectives about ourselves, others, and life are inoperable while experiencing Meditation Awareness because Observing Awareness is free from Active Mind. Our insights are simple, direct and without bias or history. I call this the "mirror quality" of meditation.

In time, we will eventually see that our direct insights into our psychological, physical and behavioral patterns naturally change those patterns without any additional effort on our part. Simply by directly seeing ourselves we change ourselves. Yet during meditation we have no goal of changing anything, which is exactly why we see ourselves clearly! It is the ultimate paradox.

It's Never to Late to Do Nothing Stage

Once we learn to meditate just to meditate, and we see for ourselves that meditation offers us much more than we originally conceived or hoped for, we start to become familiar with our practice. It becomes a personal practice, an art form.

Sometimes we feel energized at this stage of practice because we have gotten beyond the first hurdle and it has filled us with enthusiasm and a sense of freedom. None of this is an illusion. It is genuine progress. But as we soon learn, Active Mind is built on seeking pleasure, avoiding pain and ignoring everything else.

Active Mind endlessly distorts our perceptions of our self and our practice by creating many false hopes, unnecessary disappointments and dramas along the way. It has an uncanny way of ignoring the sheer simplicity of Meditation Awareness which is always present and self-evident. We must learn to escape the clutches of Active Mind's crazy creations, creations I call "crazy mind," by not reacting to them. This is why it is never too late to do nothing.

Crazy Mind

Crazy Mind is a natural byproduct of Active Mind. The central hub of Active Mind is ego, who we think we are.

Our senses and mind coordinate their processes to organize a fixed impression of the world around us and who we believe ourselves to be.

However, life is constant change. Any fixed idea of our self that we create is automatically in conflict with the nature of life. We guide our lives by our thoughts and our thoughts are products of the past.

Think about it.

We have an experience. Let's say we taste an avocado. While we are processing our sensual impressions of putting the fruit into our mouth, the first thing we encounter is a flash of pure experience.

The raw sensual reality of avocado in mouth.

At this point there are no associations, nothing to compare with what we are tasting. There is just pure experience. We can also call our experience awareness. Our experience is so immediate, so *now*, it is pure awareness.

Next, our mind, conditioned by our personal history, reels out a web of associations and relationships that match up with our raw experience of what we just tasted.

These associations and relationships rule out some things and match up others. Eventually mind identifies the experience by giving it a name, "Avocado" and ego automatically places it in one of three categories: avocado is either something we desire, dislike, or ignore.

Our raw experience was in the present moment but everything else was a product of our past right up through our reaction.

We habitually react to our moment by moment experiences through our personal history. This simple redundant vicious circle of awareness (experience), perception, feeling and reaction creates ego, which is a predictable collection of impressions of our self and the world.

The continuity of becoming aware of any object, perceiving it, having predictable impressions about it and reacting in a habitual way, makes life predictable and gives the impression that we are a solid person. We know who we are and so do others.

On an experiential level we are very much alive and sentient but our mind - who we believe we are and what we believe about the world - is purely mechanical and completely based on our past impressions.

Everyone's ego, which is developed by Active Mind and Perceptual Awareness working together, exists in a state of continuous stress between what is occurring now as raw experience and how we perceive, think, feel and react to now.

It is as if one part of human awareness is chugging along processing raw experiences as we become aware of what is happening now and another part of our awareness is frantically trying to repackage everything into something we already know. From this perspective we can say that *ego is stress* by definition.

Ego's sense of identity becomes even more rigid through the additional stress it creates by seeing itself as a literal reality. Ego is endlessly threatened by such harsh facts as the incongruities between what it believes and what is, other people's conflicting impressions and the unavoidable enemies of death and impermanence.

Ego is stress and it's naturally occurring offspring is Crazy Mind. We all have our own personal distortions of reality and they produce some creative things and some problematic things.

Our distortions, misunderstandings and confusions often cause us to see ourselves, the world, people and situations in new ways. They are very creative and progressive.

These same distortions, misunderstandings and confusions also cause us many personal and social problems and complications. They are rigid, defensive and maladaptive.

A big piece of developing a personal meditation practice is our relationship with Crazy Mind. As we meditate, our awareness of our own psychological, physical and behavioral patterns will expand further and further and we may not always like what we see.

Ego's distortions have protected us for a long time and seeing ourselves as we are is often uncomfortable at first. The saving grace in our situation is that judgement towards our self and others is only a product of ego. It has no ultimate ground to stand on. The more we regularly experience Meditation Awareness the less we hear its useless unhelpful chatter.

Our lack of criticism towards ourselves, others, and the world isn't due to being naively positive or ignoring the facts. It is due to our new ability to bridge our raw experience of now with our past impressions from our personal history.

The more experience we gain with Meditation Awareness the less seriously we take our self, our impressions and our personal history.

Ego takes a more fluid and balanced stance towards the now and we start finding it easier to coordinate body and mind in the here and now, which in turn balances our life.

Compassion becomes our guiding light because compassion neutralizes all the errors of Crazy Mind without violence. Compassion infuses our raw experience of now with Meditation Awareness allowing us to convert Crazy Mind into enlightened mind. Enlightened mind is Crazy Mind informed by Meditation Awareness through and through.

CHAPTER 9

EXPERIENCE

⊨⊪ ⊪⊨

Talking about mindfulness meditation is often problematic and complicated. For one thing, we don't have anything like meditation in Western culture. Even when we say we are "meditating on God" for instance, we are really talking about contemplation. We are taking time to think about God. In mindfulness meditation we don't think about anything and yet our minds are anything but blank.

You can discuss meditation as a technique or you can try to understand the purpose of meditation practice, but neither of these adequately capture its essence.

Some people like to learn about the religious contexts of meditation. Such studies are helpful to clarify personal experiences but they can easily turn into dry intellectualism or articles of faith, which are useless. Some folks are totally preoccupied with understanding doctrines and philosophy but have no direct experience of the things they explain.

I believe the best way of learning meditation is through personal experience. You do the practice on a daily basis. Then you have your own experiences as a reference when you discuss your practice or read the classic Yogic and Buddhist writings on meditation.

Traditionally, mindfulness meditation has been attributed to Buddha although it may have been practiced in one form or another amongst the yogis of his time. There have been many different styles of meditation practiced in India for millennium.

The original Sanskrit word for meditation is "dhyana." Dhyana can be translated as a practice leading to direct experience and realization of a deep awareness of unity that includes our perception, mind, body, senses, and environment, but is unidentified with any of them. This is Observing Awareness!

Some of the meditation styles during Buddha's time emphasized intense concentration with the goal of keeping the mind at one point, such as a location on the body, a sacred repeated word or the breath.

The goal was to neutralize all mental impressions and experience mind in its original unconditioned state. It was these forms of meditation that Buddha rejected after years of intense effort practicing them.

There are other styles of meditation that take a different approach. They also use sacred words, areas of the body and the breath as grounding devices, but the goal is different from trying to still the thought waves of the mind through concentration.

These techniques emphasize awareness of what we are experiencing in our everyday world and do not require strenuous concentration. We don't need to be an ascetic or mountain yogi, or live any particular lifestyle to practice them.

Rather than stilling the mind with the goal of experiencing something transcendental, these meditation techniques teach us to become acutely aware of our own moment by moment experiences of mind, body, senses and environment. This simple direct approach allows us a rare opportunity to witness ourselves and the world as we are.

Paradoxically, the more we become aware of our own moment by moment experiences the more we become aware of the part of our awareness that transcends those experiences and observes them.

Buddha became enlightened sitting under a tree where he had been sitting in meditation for many hours. He was very determined about his practice and vowed not to stop meditating until he attained "Nirvana," one of the original Sanskrit words for enlightenment, meaning "freedom," "extinguishing suffering."

His enlightenment, or "awakening" as it is also called, was as much an experience as it was an understanding. Buddha's enlightenment was not merely an intellectual insight into the nature of reality. He did not offer the world a belief system or religion, as we usually think of philosophies and religions.

Through the practice of meditation we are awakened from our past conditioning and our personal experience of this awakening produces a new understanding of life. An understanding that redefines our experience of life. We become reoriented to ourselves and the world.

In mindfulness practice, awakening is waking up to things as they are. We don't have a premeditated idea of reality or of life, trying to fit our experiences into it. That would simply be another form of Active Mind - ego. We experience ourselves and our environments as they are.

Although enlightenment is not the goal of many meditators today, it is still important to recognize that Buddha's enlightenment was fundamentally an experience and that his experience is understandable and accessible.

"Experience" is kind of a dirty word in our culture unless you are referring to a person's expertise, such as when someone says: "Katie has years of experience in program development; she can do anything!"

Experiences are ephemeral. They are temporary and have little substance. In our society, experiences are the equivalent of bubbles and froth on the surface of a raging river - no big deal. If someone shares a spiritual experience, people roll their eyes and consider the person naive and childish.

In our culture, if you want to do something valuable you "get down to the bone." Experiences are seen as frivolous; physiology is real, hardcore.

But in mindfulness meditation experience is everything. When we experience Meditation Awareness while meditating we are experiencing our own human natural condition.

Our mind and body are coordinated causing our stress to loosen, our breath to deepen, our mind to sharpen and our body to relax.

In this case, experience isn't fleeting or superficial. It is the natural outcome of being in a state of balance and it can teach us how to live.

It is through experiencing Meditation Awareness over and over again, that we fine tune our mind and body to a permanent state of coordination and balance, resulting in the perfect lifestyle for who we are.

This perfect lifestyle is not a contrived lifestyle. If we have the thought: "I will start living healthy! I will do such and such and stop doing this or that!" it is an idea we are creating. The perfect lifestyle arises spontaneously through regular contact with Meditation Awareness.

The balanced lifestyle we discover by meditating is the natural outcome of experiencing our self in our own perfectly balanced, perfectly natural condition.

Usually our mind and body are completely out of sync with one another. Our Active Mind is going in all sorts of directions at once and correspondingly our body is out of balance trying to compensate.

Active Mind may be hyper-jumping from task to task on our endless to-do list, as our breath is shallow and fast and our body tense and restless.

On the other hand Active Mind may be dull and unfocused, in which case our breathing is labored and our body lethargic and heavy.

There are endless combinations and possibilities when our mind and body are uncoordinated.

Imagine Active Mind as the head of a frog jumping from one chaotic direction to another, while our body is the legs of the frog frantically jumping, trying to keep up.

The condition of coordination and balance between our body and mind determines our experience of the moment. Our experience of the moment determines our coordination and balance between body and mind. One drives the other.

When we experience coordination between body and mind on a habitual basis through experiencing Meditation Awareness, we start to live exactly as we are, in balance, naturally, spontaneously.

From my viewpoint, this is wisdom. Wisdom is living optimally, spontaneously, without self-conscious effort. The result is living a stress free life. Being in balance, living optimally, being who we are, is our natural condition.

CHAPTER 10

THE PRACTICES

⟛

I n this section of the book, there is a description of four essential meditation and yoga practices. I will explain their purpose and philosophical framework. These particular four practices were chosen because they are the pillars of yoga and meditation. You may feel a connection to all of them or just some of them. The goal for each of these practices is the same. They are four roads that lead exactly to the same mountain top.

What are The Four Essential Practices?

1. Mindfulness Meditation
2. Devotion Meditation
3. Compassion Meditation
4. Selfless Service

What is the common goal of The Four Essential Practices?

Mindfulness meditation, devotion meditation, compassion meditation, and selfless service are all techniques. Whatever the particulars of each technique might be: mindfully breathing, using visualizations, repeating mantras, forming intentions, etc., they are not considered to be ultimate reality or religious doctrine.

The experiences you derive from these techniques lead to spiritual knowledge, which is defined as a combination of personal experience and understanding. Spiritual knowledge always contains both experience and understanding. Spiritual knowledge expands and strengthens our ability to link with Spiritual Intelligence.

The way I've come to understand spirituality is simple: do not accept anything on blind faith. We practice a technique that gives us the experience of Meditation Awareness. After continued practice, we become anchored in our experience of Meditation Awareness, making it permanent. Simultaneously, we learn classical yoga and meditation wisdom which clarifies our personal experience.

As the Active Mind is the seat of ego, the spiritual heart is the seat of God. In terms of our personal experience, spiritual heart is defined as a perfect balance between Observing Awareness and Active Mind - what we call Meditation Awareness.

The mind is the seat of fear, anxiety and stress. The heart knows no fear, no anxiety and no stress. It is anchored in Meditation Awareness which leads to the experience of Openness, Honesty, Dharma and Trust. These together are the same as love, the ground being of all existence. All fear, anxiety and stress are products of mind creating the illusion of duality, or "self" and "other." If there is no duality, there is no fear.

A Matter of Perception

The practice of mindfulness meditation approaches the experience of Meditation Awareness as the formless and the practice of devotion approaches Meditation Awareness as form or God.

The end experience is the same but the starting points are completely different. Combining the two types of practices is very beneficial for many people.

In the same way, compassion can be used in the place of devotion for those who are not naturally inclined towards the idea of God.

Compassion connects us to all beings without exception and so does loving God, when God is perceived within the light of our personal experience of Meditation Awareness rather than ego's projections. In light of Meditation Awareness, God exists within and without, as everyone.

It is our personal awareness of our infinite connection to all life that transforms our consciousness, not the language, technique or approach we use.

Selfless service naturally occurs as we integrate our experience of Meditation Awareness into our actions. The more regularly we experience Meditation Awareness the more our identification transfers from ego to Meditation Awareness.

We start to recognize that our usual assumptions about who we are become limited, since they only include our body and thinking emotional mind.

But Meditation Awareness includes Active Mind and Observing Awareness, the totality of human experience and consciousness.

We are not just our thoughts, emotions, sensual impressions and behaviors. We are fundamentally pure awareness. This awareness precedes, permeates, and transcends our thoughts, sensual impressions, emotions, and actions.

In both meditation and yoga our sense of who we are transfers from being a limited personality to the state of Meditation Awareness itself. We continue to be the person we have always been, but our new experience of Meditation Awareness frees us to be truly ourselves. It aligns us with Spiritual Intelligence.

As we become identified with Meditation Awareness we start to see that ego is not the cause of harmonious effective action and is not responsible for the behaviors that bring happiness to ourselves and others. It is the cause of our problematic behaviors.

Harmonious effective action is created by and executed by Meditation Awareness. Ego has a very limited perspective and therefore it creates minimal ineffective results. Meditation Awareness is full awareness and therefore it creates wide spectrum harmonious results that benefit everyone. This is selfless service.

Feel free to experiment with the four meditation techniques discussed in this book, but be aware they all require dedication, regularity, and passion before they give their gifts to you. Eventually, you will learn to do some or all of them with love and a deep appreciation and only then will your meditation become an art. When practice is art it is no longer seeking a result. Instead, it becomes our expression of attainment.

Meditation is Yoga: Yoga is Meditation

Throughout this book I use the terms "meditation" and "yoga" interchangeably. Some explanation is necessary.

Today, everywhere we look in the media and in our communities, we find people teaching, practicing or commenting on yoga and meditation. Many speak of them as distinct practices, different from one another. This is because yoga and meditation are presented as brands. However, this is a new phenomenon; it was not always so.

It seems that most of these people represent different schools of meditation and yoga of which there are innumerable traditions, developed over millenniums, starting in India and spreading throughout Asia.

Even here in America, after only a century since Buddhist and Yogic meditation was introduced into our culture, we already see new schools and traditions developing.

However, we must ask ourselves a necessary practical question: Are all these traditions really that much different from one another?

There are obvious differences between languages, techniques, imagery, explanations, rituals and cultural nuances, but are there really significant differences in the experience and knowledge they deliver?

The experience of yoga and meditation are essentially the same: beginning with yoga as taught in Bhagavad Gita, moving through Vedanta, Buddhism, and Shivaism into Taoism and Zen.

Their essence is the same.

They differ only when comparing a superficial understanding of their different practices and philosophies but not in the direct experience of reality or the knowledge and wisdom they offer.

Through my own understanding and experience, looking out over the landscape of the history of meditation and yoga, I do not see different schools and traditions. I see one wave of enlightenment moving from culture to culture, adapting to each cultural transition as required. All schools and traditions are cultural transitions of the same experience and message over thousands of years.

Next time you see one of the world's beautiful statues of Buddha sitting in deep meditation, remind yourself that Buddha is seated in a yoga posture or "asana" as it is called in Sanskrit.

The Full Lotus is one of yoga's primary asanas. It aligns body, breath, mind and environment so that Meditation Awareness can be expressed both within the person who is meditating and to all beings. Many Hatha Yoga Masters have stated that the Full Lotus is yoga's highest attainment.

Many years later, Dogen, a Japanese Buddhist monk who brought Zen from China to Japan, placed great emphasis on the importance of sitting in meditation as Buddha sat. Sitting in Zazen meditation (Full Lotus) he taught was enlightenment itself.

The same is true of yoga. At first, each asana we learn is a practice. But in time, the asana becomes both our inner experience of yoga, which means "union" or the experience of unity, and an expression of yoga from our true Self - enlightenment that radiates to others.

Why Sitting Mindfulness Meditation is Essential

Although all the essential four practices awaken the same experience, the same insight within us, I recommend sitting mindfulness meditation to everyone as their foundational practice. There are two reasons for this.

First, sitting mindfulness meditation is a solitary practice. We are left alone with ourselves. It is much easier to recognize our reactions to meditating as projections of our past conditioning when we are interacting only with our self.

It is through our recognition of our own projections that we first see the light of Observing Awareness. When we see all of our reactions to meditation are based on our past impressions, we wake up from the dreamworld of our conditioning and recognize the one thing that lies beyond all conditioning: Observing Awareness.

The second reason why sitting mindfulness meditation is so important is that experiencing Meditation Awareness, which is experiencing Active Mind and Observing Awareness simultaneously, is a prerequisite for all the other practices: devotion, compassion and selfless service.

For example, let's look at the difference between Devotion Meditation before and after the experience of Meditation Awareness (The same can be applied to Selfless Service and Compassion Meditation).

If we have never experienced Meditation Awareness and we worship God, we are always interacting with our imaginings of God through either our past conditioning or the conditioning of others. We never experience God directly because we do not know our self beyond our conditioning.

In such a situation everything we think, know, and feel about God, no matter how sincere, only exists in the limited realms of our thoughts and emotions.

After we have gained some experience of Meditation Awareness our devotion radically effects our experience of now.

God and our love for God become one force that enlivens our body, mind, and environment. Our refined emotions towards our beloved infuse our experience of the moment. They become part of the here and now. We become beacons of God's love.

Our experience of Meditation Awareness along with our refined feeling of love, join together creating an experience of our self as Observing Awareness and everything else: mind, body, emotions, Perceptual Awareness, and environment as blissful self-existing energy.

From a yogic and meditative perspective this is the way things exist. God, our true self, Observing Awareness, eternally radiates love, whose blissful energy manifests as all life forms. This is the pinnacle of Meditation Awareness and mature devotion.

I encourage you to try all four essential practices and to continue with the ones that feel natural. It is recommended that you do so while practicing sitting mindfulness meditation regularly.

CHAPTER 11

MINDFULNESS MEDITATION INSTRUCTIONS

We have already learned quite a bit about mindfulness meditation and the goal of experiencing Meditation Awareness.

We have learned how our minds continually follow a simple process that cultivates awareness of everything perceived, both inside ourselves and outside in the world, as we go about our daily activities:

1. We become aware of something, either inside ourselves or outside ourselves, such as a feeling of impatience or the smell of summer rain.

2. We build a perception of our object of awareness, using the senses and the mind, in a process called Perceptual Awareness. Both the object we are perceiving and ego, our sense of being a particular person, rises in our awareness simultaneously.

3. We have a feeling about the object we perceive based on ego's experiences of similar objects, which we have called "impressions."

4. We have a reaction towards the object of our perception, thus reinforcing our past impressions and continuing them into the future. Our reactions, based on our past impressions, maintain ego and insure we keep reacting in the same ways to objects of perception, remaining as we have always been.

This entire process takes place in what is called Active Mind, which includes all sensory information, as well as our thoughts, emotions, dreams and dreamless sleep states. Everything that enters Active Mind is transitory. It comes and goes, but ego makes it appear concrete, real and enduring.

Mindfulness meditation is a simple technique that opens our awareness so we can witness the transitory nature of everything we perceive and the transitory nature of ego.

As we become aware of our sensual impressions, thoughts, emotions, and physical sensations, as they arise in our field of awareness and pass out of our awareness, we spontaneously become aware of Observing Awareness.

Observing Awareness is a feeling of observing or witnessing everything without involvement.

With continued meditation practice, we are able to experience Active Mind and Observing Awareness together. At first, we can only do this during meditation. But with practice, we will be able to experience Meditation Awareness effortlessly throughout our day.

Choosing your Seat

How you sit for meditation is important. It significantly enhances or hinders your meditation experience.

Sit in a comfortable position, either on the floor or in a chair.

If on the floor, use a meditation pillow (such as a zafu) to sit on, so that your hips are higher than your knees, either comfortably crossed legged or kneeling, straddling the pillow. It helps to have a mat or cushion underneath you such as a zabuton mat.

If you choose a chair, make sure your feet are flat on the floor in-line with your knees. Using a firmer chair works better than a softer chair. Do not sit with legs outstretched or your feet tucked under your seat. Do not cross your legs.

The goal is to be alert, stable and comfortable. Do not choose a sitting position that will cause too much pain or will cause parts of your body to lose circulation. Using smaller support pillows to prop your body is perfectly fine.

Posture

Sit up straight but not stiff or rigid.

Your torso should be uplifted and your spine lengthened so that they naturally feel elongated.

The top of your head is naturally inline with your spine and it should feel like it is effortlessly being pulled towards the ceiling or sky.

Your chin should be slightly pulled inward towards your neck. This will help straighten your head and neck without straining either.

Your body should feel securely grounded on the earth or chair but not straining. When the body trusts its position the mind quiets automatically because it stops struggling to gain balance. Your entire sitting posture should feel trusting.

Hand Position

Using a formal hand position helps keep you centered and focused. There are two hand positions or "mudras," we recommend.

Chin Mudra

Touch your thumb and forefinger together on each hand and place palms down on your thighs or knees. Your upper arms remain inline with your torso, close to your body. Your arms and hands should feel relaxed, with no effort or strain.

Dhyana Mudra

Place your left hand on top of your right hand with fingers naturally extended and the palms facing upwards. Touch thumbs gently. Your hands rest in your lap, close to your body, near your belly. Your hands and fingers should feel relaxed without strain.

The mudra description is a guideline, not something to try and get perfect. It is acceptable to simply fold your hands if these mudras are not helpful for you. The main idea is to intentionally place your hands a specific way that is loose and comfortable, but also defined to help the attention stay alert.

Eyes

Your eyes should be loosely open or half closed glancing downward about two feet in front of you. Use an open gaze, not focusing on anything in particular. If you have excessive eye strain or if it feels too uncomfortable to keep the eyes open, you can gently close your eyes.

The Technique

Now you are ready to meditate.

Mindfulness meditation is the art of awareness. There is no concentration in this practice. The technique will result in awareness of everything that is occurring, within and without, as it occurs.

It is pure, open awareness.

Take a slow, deep breath in, filling your belly, and a long breath out, releasing the air naturally. Repeat.

Allow your breathing to return to its normal pace. Become aware of the feeling of your body and your breath as you sit comfortably.

Now become aware of the sensation of the breath as it enters and exits your nostrils. For some, its easier to feel the breath pass against their upper lip. Do not try to change your breathing in any way. Just continue to notice the sensation of the breath going in and out of your nostrils. Feeling this point of contact is your anchor. It remains constant throughout the meditation session.

While you continue to practice this, include the feeling of your body. Notice how your body physically feels while you notice your breathing. We are not trying to change anything, we are simply noticing what is.

Continue to notice your breath and your body, and include any sounds you hear in your environment. As you notice various sounds, be aware of how they come and go. Do not concentrate on the sounds, or intentionally identify them. Just include whatever you hear with the feeling of your breath and the awareness of your body.

While you are aware of your breath, your body and sounds in the environment, also be aware of your thoughts. Your thoughts are part of what is occurring right now, so you do not want to block them out. You are just becoming aware of what naturally occurs every moment of your life.

Allow your thoughts to arise and pass. Think about whatever comes into your mind. If feelings come up, allow them to be there.

Notice your mental activity. Do not resist anything. However, include your breath and anything else you are noticing in this moment.

If you are only focusing on your thoughts, you have slipped into concentration on your thoughts. When you notice this has happened, simply include the breath, be aware of your body and hear the sounds in your environment.

As you continue to sit for meditation and feel your breath, notice sounds, sights, tastes, smells, sensations, emotions and thoughts as they naturally come and go. Mindfulness is the art of noticing the ever-changing quality and impermanence of all our experiences.

The insight gained from noticing the impermanent nature of everything in your field of awareness automatically reveals Observing Awareness. Gradually, your experience of Observing Awareness will equal your awareness of Active Mind, resulting in Meditation Awareness, which is mindfulness.

Practical Tips

I recommend twenty minutes of meditation every day. You may increase or decrease this suggested time on a daily basis but practice at least twenty minutes every day on the average every week.

Use a timer to prevent becoming preoccupied by how much time has passed.

It is helpful to create a ritual with your meditation practice. Wear the same clothes to meditate, use the same space to sit, try to practice the same time each day.

CHAPTER 12
COMPASSION MEDITATION

━┿ ┿━

C ompassion is not simply an emotion, nor is it purely empathy, as often defined. Compassion is reality. We are all interrelated in this infinite universe. Two fish in the sea may experience themselves as two distinct separate entities, but those of us standing on the shore know they are both parts of the same ocean.

Compassion is our human way of acknowledging our mutual interdependence. We all arise together in this infinite universe and we all exist together. Through compassion meditation we enliven our connection to all life forms by intentionally sending them loving kindness.

Our feelings of loving kindness accompanied by our growing experiences of Meditation Awareness combine to create a web of radiating awareness and love. With Observing Awareness as our core identity, our web of compassion is egoless loving kindness or infinite loving energy.

We eventually come to see through our own experiences of Meditation Awareness and radiating compassion that our inner state is reality. Life is one. Life is love. Life is compassion. Life is self existing consciousness and energy.

Compassion Meditation Instructions

1. Take a comfortable seated meditation posture. If you have developed a mindfulness meditation practice you may practice compassion meditation for a designated time along with mindfulness meditation as follows.

2. Sit for mindfulness meditation, as explained in our Mindfulness Meditation Instructions, for approximately five minutes.

3. After your brief mindfulness meditation, close your eyes and envision someone you love or someone to whom you feel close standing before you.

4. With each inhalation imagine breathing in their suffering and pain in the form of black smoke. With each exhalation imagine sending them compassion and loving kindness in the form of white cloud. You may begin by intentionally inhaling and exhaling but after a minute or two simply breathe naturally.

5. With each inhalation you take away a little more of their suffering and with each exhalation you fill them a little more with loving kindness and happiness.

6. Now, do the same for one person whom you hardly notice in your personal life such as a grocery clerk.

7. Now, do the same for one person you do not like, someone with whom you have conflict or problems.

8. Now, imagine yourself breathing in everyone's suffering in the form of black smoke and relieving everyone's suffering with white clouds of loving kindness.

9. End by letting go of your vision and practicing mindfulness meditation for five minutes.

Starting and ending compassion meditation with sitting mindfulness meditation has several benefits. Our mindfulness practice stops us from becoming attached to the results of our compassion meditation.

It is important to distinguish between compassionate loving kindness and an ability to solve the problems of others. We are able to feel loving kindness for others naturally with practice. We are not always able to fix people's problems.

Likewise, the same is true for any desire or intention we have in life. Desire and intention are both necessary to progress in life but we must learn to use them without self-defeating attachment.

When we use the word "attachment" we are referring to our dependence on results. We become much more effective, efficient, and stress free when we do whatever we are doing with complete presence and we are not preoccupied with obtaining a specific result.

It is fine to start an action with a desire for a result but then we must let go of that preoccupation and plunge into the action for the sake of the action itself. This is a part of Dharma as we discussed in Chapter Four.

Another benefit of beginning and ending our compassion meditation practice with mindfulness is it teaches us sustained effortless loving kindness.

As we alternate mindfulness meditation with feeling love and compassion, the two become fused. Our core center of Observing Awareness radiates our positive feelings of compassion through our mind, our emotions, our body and our environment. The longer we practice, the more this fused state becomes our core state of being.

CHAPTER 13
DEVOTION MEDITATION

⊨⧾ ⧾⊨

B hakti Yoga uses devotion as its method to enlightenment. As discussed in Chapter Four, when I refer to enlightenment, I am talking about the permanent experience of Meditation Awareness.

The goal of bhakti is to attain union with God. In Western religions union with God isn't a possibility. God is uniquely God and humanity is uniquely human and never the twain shall meet. The best one can hope for is redemption and a place in God's heavenly kingdom in the future.

Fortunately, Western religion's perspective of God and human-kind is only a product of thinking mind. In other words, the reason people believe we are separate from God is because our thinking mind creates duality," self" and "other."

This mind-creation is useful when it comes to functioning and communicating on our planet. We require a sense of being a separate person to survive. Much of our progress as a species is due to a combination of humankind's sense of ego and intellect.

These evolutionary attributes also create most of our problems, such as believing we are isolated from each other and the rest of our planet and universe. This has tragically led to religious conflicts, hyper-competition, crime, war, disease, climate change and many other problems.

Bhakti Yoga teaches that God is inherently the self of all living creatures. Therefore, union with God is a natural aspect of our fundamental nature.

There are many rituals, activities, styles, and methods of worshipping God that span our planet. It is fine to use any of them in bhakti yoga or simply develop your own way of worshipping.

What bhakti yoga encourages us to do is add the experience of Meditation Awareness to our worship and rethink God through our experiences.

If you follow a religion, I am not asking you to change your religion. I am asking you to rethink your idea of God in light of your own meditation experiences.

Rethinking God

In Chapter Five we contemplated Spiritual Intelligence. Spiritual Intelligence has two features: the idea that everything is always perfect exactly as it is and the idea of spiritual evolution. We will now expand our contemplation further.

Let's look at Spiritual Intelligence a little closer and add the concept of God to it. How would God create the world and all of the universes in terms of Spiritual Intelligence?

God starts from a condition of infinite equipoise, infinitely unaware of Himself. We can call His condition at this point, a vacuum state. It is beyond all qualities.

From the depths of his infinite being arises a desire to become infinitely self-aware. God wants to know Himself through and through.

Everything we see in nature, every single entity, sentient and non sentient, all exist as temporary forms of infinite God evolving towards infinite self-awareness.

Each form is born or created into a unique state of forgetfulness. It has no knowledge of its infinite origin or infinite destiny. It has no knowledge that it is God seeking for full awareness of Himself.

As all life evolves, all life forms evolve and eventually God, in his eternal pursuit to know himself, becomes human. His brain and nervous system abilities have reached their pinnacle and are now capable of enlightenment or infinite self-awareness.

Everything you experience in your life as a human is both your experience, in terms of who you think you are, and God's experience as He experiences Himself through you as an aspect of His infinite potentiality.

At a specific tipping point, God as human, starts searching for lasting fulfillment. In his pursuit he tries everything. Some things bring him pleasure; some things bring him pain; most things bring him both pleasure and pain and all things He pursues are temporary.

As He searches for something eternal, something that will not pass away, he explores religion, whose purpose is to share with people symbols and ideas of eternal truth. For God, in His unconscious state of forgetfulness, these symbols and ideas are really projections of his own Being lost in forgetfulness.

Since religion is primarily a language and a formality that exists on the level of mind and emotion, "Heaven" which is symbolic for union with God or enlightenment, always exists in the future as a mere hope.

Each form of God passes through countless lives, practicing countless faiths, gathering partial experiences and glimpses of God.

Remember, through the lens of Spiritual Intelligence, forms of God do not have "souls" per se as we are used to hearing about in Middle Eastern religious philosophy. Each form is an expression of God. From creation, all the way through the end of the universe as we know it, only God exists in different stages of forgetfulness.

Eventually, every form of God enters a path, has an experience, meets a person or discovers a technique that awakens in him or her the experience of infinite consciousness. In rare cases, this happens spontaneously without an apparent cause.

An enlightened human being, one who has achieved union with God, can also be perceived as God fulfilling His original desire for infinite Self Awareness. Traditionally, this is the reason why recognized enlightened persons have been held in such high esteem.

This Yogic version of creation and evolution challenges some of our most basic concepts of God and life. We do not need to accept it literally in order to benefit from some of its key ideas.

For example, biblical creation stories depict God as being separate from His creation.

But is an infinite God or infinite Being really separate from anything? Doesn't "infinity" by definition imply absolutely everything?

If infinity creates everything, and if it is everything, what does it create with? Spiritual Intelligence tells us that infinity creates everything out of itself infinitely.

In such a scenario, God creating the universe is much more like a spider building a web out of his own body than an old Greek god like Zeus creating a world out of thin air.

Yet our biblical stories have much more in common with Zeus than with any modern understanding of infinity or the universe. That is because both of these stories were written around the same time in the same general geographical area.

The point of comparing our typical Western ideas about God and creation to Yogic ideas about God and creation is to increase our awareness of how we approach God with devotion.

We all begin devotional meditation with some concept of God. Our idea of God effects our initial experiences during devotion meditation.

Western notions of God imagine God as separate from all creation. There is "God" and there is His "creation."

Although there are also themes of redemption, salvation, and heaven, intimating union with God, all these themes exist in time and require God's intervention. We are left with the conclusion that God is forever divided from us by nature and therefore we experience Him that way.

But when we experience Meditation Awareness, we become aware of the inexorable unity of all life. We recognize that only the human intellect divides life into "me" and "you," "us" and "them," "God" and "creation." Duality exists on the relative level of life and not on the ultimate level. We know this from our own meditation experience.

If we love God as a separate being, our feelings of love for God will not transmute into palatable energy, as they do when we love God as being both transcendental and fully present.

In the Yogic version, God is transcendental and imminent. Our experience of Meditation Awareness is the same: Observing Awareness is transcendental and Active Mind is imminent. Our experiences of Meditation Awareness confirm Yogic descriptions of God.

In the Western model of God, we love The Lord and hope to share His company someday in heaven. In the Yogic model of God we reach complete union with The Lord as soon as we exhaust our impressions, including our impressions of God.

Once our impressions have been seen through with direct insight from Meditation Awareness we recognize our self and all beings as eternally existing within God as consciousness.

Of course, even if we begin the practice of bhakti yoga believing that ourselves and God are eternally separate from one another by design, our belief exists only on the level of mind.

As we love God more and more, deeper and deeper, our love will dissolve all of our impressions of God and our self being separate. Pure love for God is union with The Lord but it does no good to believe such an idea. We must experience it for ourselves.

If you feel a connection with devotion meditation, spend time each day in worship and meditation and observe how your feelings of love and your experiences of Meditation Awareness combine.

You do not need to spend hours each day formally practicing devotion meditation. Simply spend a few minutes before or after meditation intentionally offering loving feelings to God. You can also offer loving feelings to God throughout your day.

As your experience with Meditation Awareness grows, you will naturally start offering loving feelings to God as your own formless Observing Awareness. This will not happen because of a change in your religion, beliefs or philosophy. It will occur as a natural outcome of experiencing Meditation Awareness. Observing Awareness feels like love and therefore feelings of deep devotion heighten our experience of Observing Awareness which intensifies our love.

There is no need to turn this process into a goal or into work. Your Meditation Awareness and love will join together naturally with no extra effort of your part. All you have to do is start by spending some time each day worshipping and meditating.

I have created a list of key bhakti yoga points that will support and encourage your practice and I have included a short worship practice that is meant to be performed as part of your mindfulness meditation routine, if you feel so inclined.

Becoming Absorbed in Devotion Meditation

1. The goal of Devotion Meditation is to become absorbed in your love whereby the lover and Beloved are recognized as being essentially the same.

2. The lover cannot become merged with the Beloved through exerted effort. Our very urge for unity strengthens our sense of identity keeping us separate from the Beloved.

3. Unity is achieved by erasing our feeling of separateness. We erase separateness through strong feelings of love alternating with experiences of Meditation Awareness which gives us the experience of unity. This is the true meaning and process of yoga.

4. The regular experiences of devotional love and Meditation Awareness alternating, joins us with the Beloved and all beings.

5. "God" is another word for "Life." All ideas of God are limiting and therefore cannot be representative of God, infinite being or your true self.

A Devotion Meditation

Before or after meditation focus your mind on an image of God. He or She may be a traditional image of God such as Jesus, Krishna, Ram, Shiva, Shakti or any of the many forms of the Goddess.

If you do not feel a connection to a form of God you may focus on a saint or enlightened person such as Saint Francis, Buddha, a Guru or Teacher.

Imagine your heart center as an effulgence of white light that feels intensely loving and warm. Offer your heart as loving light to whatever form of God you have chosen for your meditation.

Now imagine God as being formed out of the same light as your heart. He or She has the image of the form of God you have chosen but He or She is made out of light.

The light of your heart, that you offered to God, merges with God's form of light. As it does, God's Light Body sends rays of light back to your heart center, which brightens and feels even more love.

As you perform this visual offering of love and receive God's light of love offering in return, silently repeat His Or Her name. You may also repeat one of the many mantras from either the meditation and yoga traditions or your personal religion. Here is a a short list of mantras:

Mantras

- So Ham or Ham Sah - "I Am"

- Sat Chit Ananda - empowerment mantra, invokes confidence and joy

- Aham Brahmasmi - cultivates awareness of being one with everything

- Om Bhavam Namah - invokes all possibilities

- Om Varunam Namah - harmonizes your life with all that exists

- Om Kriyam Namah - purifies action to be in alignment with nature

- Om Vardhanam Namah - enhances dharma and the ability to serve

- Om Mani Padme Hum - invokes compassion

- Hey Ma Durga - invokes protection

- Om Gam Ganapataye Namaha - removes obstacles interfering with our progress

- Om Namah Shivaya - honors the state of Meditation Awareness; helps sustain it

- Om Shanti Shanti Shanti - invokes peace

The point of the practice is to increase feelings of refined love and to alternate the experience of those feelings with Meditation Awareness.

Devotion meditation and compassion meditation can be substituted for one another after you are acclimated to both practices.

CHAPTER 14

SELFLESS SERVICE

I n its traditional form, the Sanskrit word Seva or "selfless service" as it is known in the West, was called Karma Yoga. The word karma means action or activity and it does not have any ethical implications such as when we say: "He has good karma" or "She has bad karma." The law of the universe is simply the natural relationship between cause and effect. It is not about good and bad.

Selfless service does not mean that we sacrifice our self for others. It has nothing to do with martyrdom. Selfless service is when we perform action without any sense of being a doer.

For example, have you ever watched a stage performance where you completely forgot that you were watching a play? You were so caught up in the storyline and drama you forgot that you were an audience member and that the characters were actors?

How about watching a musical performance that was so intense and beautiful you lost awareness of everything except for the sound?

During such moments you were "selfless." You were so fully present in the moment you lost track of yourself and of the notion of "other."

When you give to others, when you express compassion, when you have the intention of making our planet a better world and you do it selflessly, you are performing selfless service.

The key is to be fully present in the moment, which is the same thing as experiencing Meditation Awareness.

Selfless service is contributing to the world and performing the action so mindfully that we give without ego, without ownership, without expectation for any specific result. In such a situation we are inspired and our intuition becomes very sharp.

We must begin with a genuine desire to be helpful and we must allow our genuine desire to be clarified and purified by the experience of Meditation Awareness.

The regular experience of Meditation Awareness is essential. Without it, what will purify our giving? What will sift ego out of our perceptions of situations and our solutions or efforts to help others? What will assure that we are making things better rather than worse?

Let's look at one example: if you are a healthcare provider such as a mental health professional, a nurse, or a physician the more you experience Meditation Awareness the more you will be able to offer your skills and knowledge to your clients without becoming attached to any particular outcome.

Attachment to outcomes is a product of ego and the thinking mind. You imagine how things should turn out, what would be best for your client but your client may not cooperate with your vision of her or his life. The conflict that you create between yourself and your client will sabotage and limit the benefits you offer him or her out of your skills and knowledge.

But if your sense of self is anchored more in Meditation Awareness than ego you allow life to take its own course and you no longer feel a need to secure any specific result. This allows your client to absorb your knowledge and skills without being pressured to conform to your notion of her or his world. It also allows you to be completely absorbed in your part of the healing process - using the skills and knowledge you have worked hard to learn - rather than being preoccupied with results, and this will optimize your ability to help. This is selfless service.

CHAPTER 15

PERSONAL GROWTH

~=+ +=~

Most of us begin meditating to improve our life. We may want to decrease our stress, improve our health, recover from addiction, end harmful habits, feel happier, become more productive and many other possibilities. In this chapter we will explore how meditation improves our lives and helps us reach our personal goals.

The experience of Meditation Awareness fosters personal growth in a completely unique way. It is a subtle process, not easy to understand at first, because it is so different from our usual method of mastering skills to obtain a specific result. A great example of this is the goal of losing weight.

If I want to lose weight I go to my physician, who will suggest specific lifestyle changes related to nutrition, diet and exercise. After I educate myself, I can make a weight loss plan and start implementing it into my daily routine.

Unfortunately, as we know from research and personal experience, my chances of maintaining my target weight are very small. Most of us do lose weight when we stick to a diet plan and regularly exercise, but in time we tend to slide back into old patterns of behavior that undo our progress. This is equally true of any other self improvement goal.

From a meditative and a yogic perspective, the scenario that I just described is perfectly natural and unavoidable. Old psychological, emotional and behavioral patterns are woven into our psyches and bodies like water permeates a wave. There is literally no way to overcome them through willpower or effort. We may keep them repressed for periods of time, but they will keep hounding us until they are allowed expression again.

Every impulse we feel originated from an impression that we once experienced in our life. Once the seed of the impression is planted into our Active Mind, ego claims it as part of its identity. Therefore giving up an impulse, an impression, is the same thing as giving up our sense of who we think we are.

Willpower or exerted effort is always a product of Active Mind. When we try to change a habit or an emotional pattern through effort, we are using the same aspect of our consciousness to defeat the pattern that created the pattern. It is like trying to lift yourself up by your shoelaces! It simply cannot be done.

However there is good news. There is another method that bypasses this inherent contradiction that always leads to defeat. The regular experience of Meditation Awareness shifts our sense of identity from ego, which is one aspect of Active Mind, to Meditation Awareness. As our sense of identity shifts, old dysfunctional patterns simply fall away. We don't defeat them. They pass away naturally like thoughts pass away during Meditation Awareness.

Everything in Active Mind is transitory and naturally arises in consciousness and passes out of consciousness, unless ego identifies with it. All we must do is meditate regularly, have compassion and love for ourselves, and let nature do the rest. Ego will let go of its identification with any impression in time.

We can take a lesson from our friend the old farmer who was wise enough to let Spiritual Intelligence defeat his fox. Whenever we try to change ourselves through personal effort we are asking our fox to catch our fox!

I would like to share six tools I have discovered throughout the years that have helped maximize the benefits I have received from meditation. Learning how to use each tool will help facilitate your meditation practice. They do not require anything more from you except understanding a few key concepts.

Tool #1: The Power of Intention

Consciousness continuously pulses between impulses of energy and impulses of stillness, alternating constantly. Every moment, our minds are either expressing energy in one form or another - through thinking or engaging in activity, for example - or balancing energetic activity with interspersing moments of stillness and silence. Back and forth, back and forth, our consciousness goes: on off, on off, ad infinitum. I visualize it like a fountain pulsating water into the air.

If we introduce our intention into the naturally occurring gaps of stillness, we can reorganize the dynamics of consciousness's system of impulses of energy.

Our activity, starting with the finest impulses of feeling and thought, transforming into desire and then behavior, starts realigning itself with our intention. This is how we change habits, addictions, and self defeating patterns in all areas of life. It is also how we reach our goals and create the life we wish to live.

If we try to change anything in our life using our current energetic impulses of consciousness, such as when we make a conscious effort towards a goal, our progress in manifesting our intention is automatically limited to the configuration of our consciousness's present conditioned patterns. "Old habits die hard" as they say.

In such a situation, which is typical for most of us, we have created a conflict between our intention and our habitual psychological and behavioral patterns. The tension between our current status and our desire for change becomes increasingly stressful and self defeating since no opposite can ever completely dominate the other.

All opposite impressions and forces whether psychological, emotional or behavioral exist together in Active Mind, either in various degrees of opposition or in various degrees of support of one another, but fundamentally they are one unit. Our mind exists as a play of opposites and no force of willpower will ever cause one opposite impression to permanently dominate or eradicate another impression.

Tool #2: Working with Opposite Impressions

If it is impossible for us to make permanent positive changes in our life through exerted effort, how do we end self defeating psychological, emotional and behavioral patterns? How do we progress towards a more fulfilling life?

As we discussed in Chapter Eight, our minds are completely mechanical. Let's say we have an experience such as walking through a shady forest on a hot summer day. We hear the cooling stream and the cicadas and we feel a deep restful sense of peace.

Our experience casts an impression on Observing Awareness which registers in Active Mind. The next time we see or think of a similar forest we will feel what we originally felt on that hot summer day.

Through this redundant system, the mind collects and connects experiences and impressions, creating a web of reactivity. This web of reactivity is the matrix of our personality and dictates what we desire, oppose and ignore. Every impression we collect creates in us either a desire, an aversion or a neutral response. We either want something, don't want something, or consider it unimportant.

When we want to neutralize an impression, such as the desire-habit to overeat, we must develop an opposite impression such as eating with contentment. When our two impressions are equal - when we can equally overeat or eat with contentment, doing both with total comfort and acceptance - the two impressions will neutralize each other. At that time, and not before, we will be totally free from our impression and our impulse to overeat will be gone forever.

This is why so many people recovering from addiction have a tendency to relapse. It is also why addiction is described as a progressive disease. Some people are able to repress their addictive impulses for years at a time. But since they haven't neutralized their impressions, the impressions that manifest into desire, when their inner dam of resistance breaks, the energy and force of their desire is overpowering.

Thankfully, it is not necessary to individually neutralize each impression that we want to transform. Impressions are endless and they each vary from person to person and situation to situation.

Whenever we experience Meditation Awareness, no matter how briefly, our impressions become neutralized. Our state of complete openness and awareness allows us to consciously contain all opposite impressions at once since we are not engaging any of them.

Meditation Awareness is never a state of exertion nor can it be experienced through personal effort. Meditation Awareness comes about through the practice of meditation and is a direct result of the technique and not our will.

Of course, we should not expect Meditation Awareness to neutralize all of our impressions immediately and completely. Our impressions lose their power over us as we stop reacting to them. Our lack of reactivity usually comes about slowly.

First, we accept our impressions and stop judging them. Then, we give up ridding ourselves of them, since any self-conscious victory over them implies they are still latent in our mind and will become active again.

When we stop trying to get rid of these unwanted tendencies we find that our impressions stop affecting us. We can take them or leave them. Slowly they start thinning out and soon they simply fall away. In some cases they remain, but we are completely comfortable with them and they no longer have power over us.

One word of caution. I am not suggesting you intentionally indulge your desires. Each and every time an impression arises in your mind and you act on the impression you encourage its strength and longevity.

I recommend you just follow your usual routine and way of living, with the simple addition of experiencing Meditation Awareness through the practice of mindfulness meditation and any of the other four essential practices. This alternation between Meditation Awareness and "life as usual" will do all the work for you.

Tool #3: Dropping the Storyline of Your Life

Everyone has a sense of who they are as a person. This sense of identity is referred to as ego and as stated earlier, ego is a combination of Active Mind and Perceptual Awareness. Our mind and senses coordinate their processes to create our sense of being a particular person with a unique storyline that we typically refer to as "my life."

As we gain more and more experience with Meditation Awareness we start to recognize a most peculiar thing. The only thing we ever experience in life is *now*. Every moment from birth until death we are only ever experiencing now.

What we call "my life," our personal storyline, which includes our perceptions about our past and our hopes for our future, is nothing but mind in the forms of memory and anticipation that are both parts of Active Mind.

Our unique human ability to engage in abstract thinking, as ingenious and helpful as it is, only exists in the now. Reality only exists now. Whatever you are experiencing right now, whatever you are doing, is the sum total of you. Your storyline is made up of a vast constellation of past impressions which are all gone. Your hopes for your future are nothing but your own projections of your past impressions.

Who we truly are is a complex, continuously changing experience of now. With each inhalation our breath takes energy into our body and with each exhalation our mind, senses and body become engaged and active. Without anticipation and memory, we are whatever we are experiencing at the moment; both anticipation and memory are only happening in the moment, always.

Herein lies an unconventional perspective of human potential. Our usual methods for changing our psychological, emotional and behavioral patterns are based on a simple mistaken perception. The strategy goes something like this: "I am a solid, concrete self with a very personable, real storyline. I need to change. I am not sufficient the way I am. I discovered a better self. This improved self does certain things and doesn't do other things. I want to be this better self so I will start doing the things this improved self does to change my life."

The inherent contradiction in this approach to changing our life is that its premise is untrue. We are not a solid literal entity and neither is this imagined improved self. And our problems in life are seldom caused by what we do or do not do. They are mostly caused through a process of mistaken identity.

Once Active Mind is balanced with our experience of Observing Awareness, ego's hold on us starts to loosen. Who we perceive ourselves to be becomes more and more adaptable, but also more grounded in the here and now.

From a meditation and yoga perspective, we change and develop our lives through the process of exhausting past impressions, not by trying to become ego's archetype of a better person. All of ego's archetypes are nothing more than replications of ego. Listening to ego is the mental equivalent of chasing your tail.

Tool #4: Body, Mind and Breath Coordination

Body and mind coordination create our moment by moment experience. As humans, we have the natural ability to consciously coordinate our bodies and minds and to effect our moment by moment experience. The simplest way to do this is through our conscious awareness of breath.

We are born with an inhalation and we die with an exhalation. Breathing is living. Peculiarly enough, we hardly ever pay any attention to our breath. In fact, we often ignore it. Our breath is the key to correct natural posture. Our breath is the key to a calm mind. Our breath is the key to greater awareness and improved concentration. Our breath is the key to improved digestion and better sleep. Our breath is the key to making better choices and to living a healthy life. Our breath is the key to thinking positive, feeling positive and making positive improvements in our life. Our breath is the key to transforming stress into creative action.

During Mindfulness Meditation our breath is our anchor. We do not concentrate on our breath, but we always include our awareness of its sensation in our nostrils while perceiving everything in our mind, Perceptual Awareness and five senses.

During meditation we are aware of our full inhalation: as we breathe in, our lower belly extends like a balloon and we feel our breath cease for a moment as our inhalation is complete before we start our exhalation.

We are also aware of our full exhalation: as we breathe out into our immediate environment, our breath pauses again as our exhalation is complete before we start our next inhalation.

Our natural effortless breathing pattern continues this cycle of inhalation, pause, exhalation, pause, and so on. Thus, breath is not constant as we may have assumed.

As we become familiar with Meditation Awareness, our full experience of breathing naturally extends into our daily activities. We don't concentrate on our breath. That would only succeed in dividing our attention between what is happening now and our self-imposed choice to focus on our breath. We are simply aware of our full breath while everything else is happening due to our meditation practice.

As being aware of breathing becomes second nature to us, we simultaneously become aware of ego being created at the beginning of each breath and ego passing away at the end of each breath. Self is a momentary thing. Seeing first hand, how every thing in human awareness is transitory, including our identity, or sense of self, transforms our moment by moment experience as well as our human potential.

We don't need to try to change ourselves any more. Nature reconfigures our life and we genuinely become ourselves, the only authentic thing we can become.

What we learn in time is that positive change is natural. It is we, through ego's tenacious clinging to old patterns, that have kept ourselves stuck. The only reason we have felt demoralized at times, because of our inability to make positive changes, is because we have been going about it all wrong.

Tool #5: Being Fully Present in the Moment

Being fully present in the moment is living Meditation Awareness in each moment. Our awareness is fully open, our senses are fully open and our thinking emotional mind is unrestricted. Being fully present also means we feel all of our feelings as they arise in the moment. Our physical sensations, our emotions and our moods are experienced and digested as they come into our awareness.

Try to think of your emotions and bodily sensations as forms of energy. They contain force and momentum. All of our emotions and sensations are immediately accompanied by either a desire, an aversion or indifference and they all compel us to internal and external actions. These impulses are energetic.

During Meditation Awareness we feel, experience and process all of our emotions and sensations on the spot as they come into existence. This means we do not wind up storing the energies of emotions and bodily sensations that we cannot satisfy through desire, avoidance or ignoring in our body.

Stored energies from unprocessed emotions and physical sensations are part of how we hold on to our past impressions. Once these energies are stored in the body our ability to satisfy them, overcome them or ignore them is nil.

However, when we live in the moment and fully experience now as it is happening, our stored up energies that exist in the forms of unprocessed feelings, emotions and moods are digested and we allow them to pass. The impressions and patterns they created will pass with them. This process does not take any further action on our part. We simply need to meditate regularly.

Tool #6: What to Do with the Mind

Our brains were made to think, to create, to interpret and to imagine. As humans, this is perfectly natural and can be incredibly rewarding. However our mind is also capable of creating all sorts of problems. As the old yoga saying goes: "The mind makes a wonderful servant and a terrible master."

One of the most common mistakes new meditators make is the assumption that their minds should go blank and that their thinking should stop.

Active Mind is always active but everything that makes up Active Mind is transitory. Our job is not to change or fix our mind. Our job is to notice the impermanent nature of everything in mind. This one seemingly small step is the catalyst for experiencing peace, happiness, letting go of dysfunctional habits, improving health and relationships and riding the wave of Spiritual Intelligence all the way to enlightenment.

When dealing with Active Mind the best strategy is simply to let it be. Learn to allow everything in your mind to come and go. This takes practice but if you meditate regularly it will become automatic to you, because in truth, everything in your mind is already coming and going. Nothing in your mind is a problem until you identify or react to it. The more you experience Observing Awareness the easier it will be to effortlessly allow all thoughts, emotions, sensations and impulses to come and go.

Ego's job is to create a sense of identity and continuity out of all the impressions contained in Active Mind. Although this is necessary for every day functioning, we mistakenly come to believe in ego's literal existence. Once we believe in ego's literal existence, Crazy Mind develops and with it all of our problems.

When we are experiencing Meditation Awareness our awareness is wide open. Our thoughts, emotions, bodily sensations and sensory input all exist as one field of constantly changing awareness.

But when we focus on an object, either an internal object such as a thought, or an external object such as a tree, Active Mind is organized by Perceptual Awareness into ego.

We cannot perceive an object without relating to it from a separate reference point and that reference point is "I." There is always "other" and "I." In truth, our real sense of being "I" or "me" is Observing Awareness. That is the true "I." Observing Awareness is our original "I."

When Perceptual Awareness is organizing sensual information along with Active Mind, to create a perception of an object, part of the process is naming the object. For example, after our senses and mind work together to create our perception of a red and green orb with a stem, the final step is to name it "apple." We always perceive everything by gathering sensual information and by naming it. Therefore thought is an intricate part of our perception.

We cannot perceive an apple or any other object without also naming our internal reference point as "I" or "me." The problem comes when we mistake the thought, "I" or "me" for Observing Awareness. Soon we lose all contact with our original internal reference point, Observing Awareness, and we relate to our self as all the thoughts we have gathered about our self from our personal history.

In Buddhist meditation schools this has been explained in the analogy "Mistaking the moon for the finger pointing at it."

Here is a quote from the Sixth Zen Patriach Huineng elaborating on this analogy:

"Truth has nothing to do with words. Truth can be likened to the bright moon in the sky. Words, in this case, can be likened to a finger. The finger can point to the moon's location. However, the finger is not the moon. To look at the moon, it is necessary to gaze beyond the finger, right?"

So ego, our sense of being who we believe and feel we are, comes into existence whenever we perceive any internal or external phenomenon, and it dissolves as soon as we stop perceiving the phenomenon. This is how ego really exists. But due to our ability to remember the past and anticipate the future through thinking, we misinterpret our sense of identity and come to believe that we are a solid concrete reality separate from the rest of the universe. This error is the breeding ground of Crazy Mind.

We don't need to get over ego, or transcend ego, or abolish ego, or improve ego, we simply need to see it as it is. This is an extremely important point because when we come to meditation, ego is very much in charge and it immediately gets to work to incorporate meditation and enlightenment into its domain of illusion.

Ego tells us that through the process of meditation we are really going to improve ourselves and our lives. We are going to become better people, maybe even special people like Buddha! Ego loves the idea of being holy and saintly in contrast to all the unholy people in the world.

Ego sees meditation as self improvement, when in fact it is self awareness. An enlightened being is not saintly or holy. An enlightened person is simply authentic and fully human. They are simply being who they are without any self conscious process.

As you meditate regularly, you will start to catch ego and its projections relating to your meditation practice. When you become discouraged and feel you are not progressing, ego has interpreted meditation as a self improvement program and has made you feel like you have failed. When you get elated at your progress, ego has interpreted progress in meditation as you becoming a special person, only deepening your misperception of yourself with who you hope to be.

114

Of course these are only two examples of ego's endless distortions. Each of us has our own unique forms of Crazy Mind that present special challenges and make us interesting creative people.

Each time we catch ego in the act of distorting reality, during the process of developing our meditation practice, we see through ego and gradually develop equanimity. We must completely accept ego and stop being perturbed by its tenacious hold on us.

Eventually ego becomes so transparent we can watch as it arises within our experience as we perceive an object, and we can watch as it dissolves as our perception of the object is complete. The process is much like the ocean's surf splashing onto the shore and receding.

At this point, the entire self conscious process of watching ourselves, evaluating ourselves, and trying to fix ourselves starts to unravel. We begin to be ourselves exactly as we are, moment to moment, grounded completely in the present.

This is true progress in meditation practice, but it isn't really progress per say because all we are doing is becoming what we have always been. It's never too late to do nothing!

The keys to working with your mind, and particularly with ego, are patience and compassion for yourself and others, as well as developing a good sense of humor. This is why people have often practiced compassion meditation, devotion meditation and selfless service along with sitting meditation. However, none of them besides mindfulness meditation are necessary.

CHAPTER 16
SECULAR SPIRITUALITY

There is a new and exciting opportunity available to all of us who live in a modern democracy. An opportunity to advance individually and as a society. An opportunity brought about by science, technology, secular social progress and our newfound understanding of ancient meditation practices, which are some of humankind's earliest and greatest discoveries in consciousness.

For the first time, humankind is able to move out of the shadows of religious superstition and into the sunlight of authentic spirituality. We are now able to replace unproven religious dogmas with genuine personal spiritual experience, and because of the rapidly progressing field of brain science, we are starting to understand the physiological effect of meditation practice on the human brain.

Soon we will be able to regain wisdom that was prevalent in the ancient world enabling us to scientifically discover why and how that wisdom optimizes our own biology and aligns our biology with the rest of nature.

My practice and understanding of the ancient wisdom outlined in this book has led me to classify this next inevitable step in social evolution as "Secular Spirituality."

This book was created to culturally transition ancient wisdom practices into Western Society and to further the growth of Secular Spirituality. This can be accomplished by helping people understand what Secular Spirituality is and teach them how to experience its countless benefits.

Imagine a society where everyone can experience true spirituality through Meditation Awareness for themselves, without their experiences being subverted to another cause such as converting the world to a particular way of living or a political agenda.

Imagine a society where we can live a spiritual life that doesn't cause all the problems that have been brought about through traditional religion.

We are capable of learning how to coordinate our own body and mind to discover spirituality's truths. Spiritual truth exists in every one of us.

By aligning our body, our breath and our awareness, we experience the full range of human consciousness and tap into Spiritual Intelligence.

Spiritual Intelligence is what naturally, spontaneously occurs within any given situation, when there is someone involved in the situation who has learned to coordinate body and mind. Someone who is acting from Meditation Awareness.

In many ways the Western World has yet to take advantage of its greatest resource: freedom. Every one of us in the United States have an unalienable right to life, liberty and the pursuit of happiness.

As it is stated in the Declaration of Independence: *We hold these truths to be self-evident, that all men are created equal, that they are endowed by their Creator with certain unalienable Rights, that among these are Life, Liberty and the pursuit of Happiness.*

Despite this historical declaration of our unique legal freedom, we continue to be culturally held back by beliefs and perspectives on life that are thousands of years old. Many of these beliefs go against logic, empathy, justice, history and science. Yet many of us live by them daily in the name of religion.

The reason we do so is simple: human beings are spiritual beings. It is our nature. Look back through history and you will discover unique forms of spirituality at the foundation of every culture.

Unfortunately, our spiritual nature has been used as a channel for others to gain power, including power over us. There is nothing more limiting, nothing that reduces freedom more, than controlling how people see themselves and the world.

We now live in a time when we can take spirituality back from the religious franchises who claim it as their own. We can experience true spirituality ourselves by using authentic spiritual practices such as mindfulness meditation and yoga without turning our experiences into dogma.

Secular Spirituality distinguishes between the experience of Meditation Awareness which is available to everyone, and each person's interpretation of their experience. That means we can each experience Meditation Awareness and we can communicate with each other about our experiences. We can also clarify our experiences of Meditation Awareness individually and as a community by reading ancient Buddhist and Yogic meditation texts.

But there is no need for us as a Secular Spiritual community, to distill our common spiritual experiences of Meditation Awareness into doctrine or to systematize our spiritual experiences into a system of beliefs.

Secular Spirituality was most likely humankind's original spirituality. A spirituality that existed before giant religious monopolies institutionalized personal spiritual experiences into their own religious doctrines.

We can have our cake and eat it too. We can develop an authentic spiritual life without becoming superstitious and without isolating ourselves from science and one another.

What is Secular Spirituality?

Secular Spirituality is the natural outcome of recognizing that all descriptions of reality are *descriptions* and that no description of reality can ever be complete or be equivalent to reality itself. We learn this when we break the code of our own mind and realize that our thoughts about things are not the things they represent.

This insight comes about through personal experience of Meditation Awareness and not through speculation or philosophy. In other words, there is a difference between understanding the idea: *our thoughts about things are not the things they represent* and personally experiencing the truth behind the idea within yourself.

To get a clearer idea of what is meant by descriptions of reality, let's look at a few common ones that people accept as being ultimate truth. Many people believe that we live once and after death we go to heaven or hell. There are others who believe we live once and die without any form of afterlife. There are others still who believe we live and die many times, taking different forms in different incarnations.

But all of these belief systems are only different descriptions of reality. They are merely symbols of the truth or "a finger pointing at the moon" as our friend the Sixth Zen Patriach Huineng told us.

They are examples of how we talk to ourselves and like-minded people about the journey of life. None of them are actually life or proven reality. They are *thoughts* about life. Life can never be described because we are life itself. We are not living life, we are life! We can no more describe what we are or the process of life than our nose can smell itself or our tongue can taste itself.

Of course, the mind will immediately ask for clarification and demand: "What is real then?" Our body and senses do not ask this question. They are content being where they are, experiencing whatever they are experiencing in the moment. Only our mind creates questions and demands answers about who we are and where we are going. Interestingly enough, these questions cannot be answered with the mind.

Is there no ultimate reality then? Are the nihilists correct when they say that reality amounts to meaningless nothingness?

Buddha described reality as "emptiness" because reality has no inherent qualities and everything that exists is dependent on causes and conditions. In this way, all phenomenon comes into existence together, relying on each other.

However, we must be careful not to attribute conventional qualities and status onto emptiness, because emptiness itself is empty.

Buddha pointed out a simple profound point that is overlooked about the human mind and how it perceives reality. Everything we know is only conventional reality. A red stop light means "stop" because we have all agreed that's what it means. There is nothing inherent in the color red that refers to stopping. In this way we build our human world.

If ultimate reality could be described in terms of conventional reality, it wouldn't be ultimate reality.

Reality can be experienced but never known. Like a massive river headed towards the ocean, we can harmonize our lives with the river course of life but we cannot stand back from it and know it like an object of our perception.

This is the simple difference between religion and spirituality. Religion claims that its description of life is an ultimate description, one that has been revealed by God and one that accurately represents reality.

But as we have seen, life cannot be contained in words. Whether the words have been divinely inspired or not doesn't change the limitations of language and thought.

Spirituality gives each participant a direct experience of reality and descriptions of that experience are secondary. They are simply conventions of speech changing from culture to culture. This is why it is perfectly possible to meditate and be either an atheist or a devout follower of any religion. The experience of Meditation Awareness is applicable to any and to all descriptions of life.

When we practice Secular Spirituality, we don't need to change our description of who we are and what we think life is all about. We only need to recognize our description of life for what it is: a description.

Secular Spirituality will reverse the trend of religion's stranglehold on spiritual experience. People will again be able to experience the full spectrum of their own consciousness.

No one will be able to take away what each person learns within themselves. The need for competition between different faiths will be seen for what it is: simple spiritual immaturity.

No lifestyle or culture will be excluded from Secular Spirituality's community. Personal freedom, self reliance and inclusivity will be the forces that spread Secular Spirituality around the globe.